Keralites on the Move

Keralites on the Move

A Historical Study of Migration from Kerala

K.V. Joseph

SHIPRA

ISBN: 81-7541-278-X

First Published in India in 2006

Keralites on the Move

Published by :
SHIPRA PUBLICATIONS
115-A, Vikas Marg, Shakarpur,
Delhi-110092 (India)
Ph. : 91-11-55277210, 22500954
Email : info@shiprapublications.com
Website : www.shiprapublications.com

Laser Typesetting by:
R.S. Prints,
New Delhi

Printed at:
Chaudhary Offset Process
Delhi-110051

Foreword

It is now very well known that the state of Kerala is both a revelation and a mystery. The revelation lies in the clear superiority of Kerala vis-à-vis other state in indicators like life expectancy, literacy, health, social consciousness etc. Yet the mystery is that the state still has not attained the state of industrialization reached by many of the other states of India. We also now know that over the last forty years (and particularly in the 70's) Kerala was the number one foreign exchange earner via its exports of skilled labour to other parts of the world.

In fact, India's severe balance of payments crisis of the past was largely mitigated by the inflows of foreign exchange from Malayalees working in Gulf countries. In addition, while not developing much as an industrial state, Kerala has been in the forefront as an exporter of skilled labour. It is in the light of this that Professor Joseph's book is a useful addition to the literature. The book tries to explain the factors behind the process of migration of Malayalees. It is noted that, contrary to what many believe, Malayalees were never fond of migrating even within India till the turn of this century.

It is argued that the Malayalees population outside the country before 1901 was negligible. More over, there was little migration of Malayalees to other parts of the country. Nor did they not move out of the country as part of indentured labour which is known to have migrated to countries like South Africa or U.K. In this context the author argues that two factors may have promoted out-migration of Malayalees in this century. First, the fact that Kerala was an important sea port. This implied that the population of Kerala interacted significantly with foreigners from diverse countries like Rome, Palestine, South-Africa, Russia and China as far back as the 16th Century. In addition, there was also in migration of other communities from other parts of India into Kerala.

Second, economic factors like development of education, media and improvements in the transportation led to socio-economic transformation of the public, making them willing to migrate to other parts. It is also argued that migration of Malayalees has not been unilateral and directed to any specific part of the world. After migration, the development conscious Malayalees have set up their own community structures in other countries and yet succeeded in integrating effectively with host countries.

With India today integrating with the rest of the world in a very meaningful way, this book is a useful addition to the literature on how societies can develop and intermingle with other cultures without losing their own social cohesion.

Prof. Manoj Pant

JNU, New Delhi
Sept. 22, 2005

Preface

With the ever increasing volume of migration in the contemporary world, diasporic studies are also on the increase in many parts of the world including India. However, no study on the migratory movements of some of the important linguistic-cum-ethnic groups has been made so far, though literature on various aspects of migration are galore in India. Malayalees who form the linguistic community of Kerala is one of such groups whose migratory movement has been a neglected area so far, though they are a highly mobile class of people in the Indian sub-continent. Keralites are to be found in fairly large numbers, not only in the metropolitan cities of India but also in foreign lands like Dubai, Abudhabi, Manama, Oman, New Jersey, Rome, Cologne etc. While some of the migrants from Kerala could occupy very high positions in foreign lands, the remittances which they send to Kerala provide a major portion of the material means required to sustain the so-called Kerala model of development.

The material means which the migrants provide through the remittances make Kerala a highly prosperous state. The posh residential buildings with all the modern fittings discernible from one end of the state to the other, the multitude of automobiles flooding the roads and the narrow lanes of Kerala, the ultra modern consumer durables and other costly articles displayed in the ever increasing number of shops in all parts of the state speak of the conditions of prosperity pervading throughout Kerala. Furthermore, in various indicators of economic performance like per capita income, per capita bank desposit or reduction in the incidence of poverty, Kerala tops among the states of India except Maharashtra and Punjab. On the other hand, the state would have been reduced to a miserable condition in the context of near stagnation of the agricultural and industrial sectors of the economy but for the inflow of remittances. It is the toils and moils of hundreds of thousands of her sons and daughters scattered in different parts of the world that make Kerala shining much better than that of the days of Mahabali, the legendary king of antiquity.

Though hundreds of thousands of Keralites work and live in distant lands, migratory movement of Keralites is comparatively of a recent development. Notwithstanding the presence of large number of pre-modern trading diasporas of the foreign merchants of West Asian or even Mediterranean origin in Malabar coast during the pre-da Gaman period, very few Keralites seemed to have moved out of Kerala at any time in the past. Travels of persons like Adi Sankara in various parts of India during the 9th century, or of Joseph the Indian in various parts of Europe during the sixteenth century etc., were basically migratory movements of mere individuals which did not evoke any interest among the people to stir out of their village moorings. However, the migratory movement which started in trickles during the closing decades of nineteenth century could gain momentum within a short period and Kerala could overtake some of the leading outmigrating states like Tamil Nadu, Andhra Pradesh, Orissa, Gujarat etc. in quick succession.

In a sense, what the contemporary Malayalees do in their migratory movement is a reverse process of what happened in the past. Kerala has been a haven of immigrants from different parts of the world from ancient past. Trading diasporas of the ancient Greeks, the Romans, the Arabs, the Jews, the Persians etc. have been established at different periods of time during the ancient period and many of them have settled down in the coastal towns of Kerala. Instances of inmigration from other parts of India are also numerous. Even the ancestors of the present Namboodiri Brahmins of Kerala are believed to be inmigrants from Maharashtra, Karnataka, Andhra Pradesh and so on. Inmigration and settlement of ethnic communities from other parts of India are also galore during the modern period. The list of such inmigrants includes the Konkani Brahmins, the Pattar Brahmins, Gujaratis, Memons, the Rowther Muslims etc. They are incorporated in the Kerala society with all privileges as the sons of Kerala, though some of them retain their linguistic identity. It is now the turn of Kerala or rather Malayalee society to send her sons and daughters to those far off places like Rome or Arabia or the Persian Gulf countries in the foreign lands or to Maharashtra or Karnataka or Tamil Nadu in other parts of India as the societies of those places did in the past.

Though the Romans or the Arabs or the Persians knew much about the topographical conditions of Kerala or its products during the ancient past, nobody has mentioned anything about the people of Kerala or any of their achievements. In all probability nobody from Kerala has made any indelible mark at any time in the past. However, the sons of Kerala could occupy exalted positions and are in a position even to shape world events once they started to move from their rustic moorings. Perhaps Kerala was too small a place for them to play their proper role in the past. Apparently, the history of Malayalee migration is the story of Malayalees emerging in the world scene in a big way and claiming their rightful place in the globalised world.

A study on the migratory movement of Keralites from the formative days would naturally be an interesting theme. The present study is an earnest attempt in that direction. The author was awarded with a Senior Fellowship by the Indian Council of Historical Research, New Delhi, for making such a study. The author takes this opportunity to record his deep sense of gratitude and indebtedness to the Indian Council of Historical Research for awarding the fellowship without which the study would not have been completed. The author is grateful to Dr. Rajkumar and Dr. B.K. Pandeya, former Dy. Directors of the I.C.H.R. for having been very helpful to the author at different stages of the tenure of the fellowship.

The fellowship was affiliated to the Centre for Development Studies, Trivandrum. The author expresses his deep sense of gratitude to the authorities of the Centre for Development Studies, Trivandrum and in particular to Dr. Chandan Mukherjee, the former Director for all the help rendered for pursuing the study to a final stage. The author also thanks to Dr. E.T. Mathew, Dr. G.N. Rao, Dr. Michael Tharakan and Dr. Irudaya Rajan, former and current faculty members of the Centre for Development Studies for offering a helpful hand to his academic pursuits at the CDS.

The present study could not be completed without utilising the materials available in the Archives at Delhi and Madras and in various well equipped libraries. In this connection, the author expresses his deep sense of gratitude and obligation to the devoted members of the staff of the CDS library under the stewardship of Sri V. Ramakrishnan,the former Librarian. Thanks are due to the staff of the Administration and Finance and Accounts Sections of the CDS.

Last but not least, the author records his heartful thanks to Ms. Girija who did a fine job of typing the final draft very neatly at very short time.

Dr. K.V. Joseph

Contents

List of Tables

Chapter 1
Introduction

The propensity to migrate to other places is as old as humanity itself. During the primitive days man had to wander from place to place in search of food. The ceaseless wanderings in search of food came to an end with the domestication of animals and the introduction of corn cultivation; two epoch making developments in the history of human civilization. Since then, a sedantry habit set in and migratory movements of the ordinary people were confined to the narrow limits of the localities which happened to be their places of habitats. However, natural calamities like droughts; political upheavels like wars; and religious persecutions very often resulted in large scale migration in different parts of the world on many occasions in the past. The exodus of the Jews or the wanderings of the Huns etc., were a few instances, of such migration. Most of those migratory movements were involuntary in nature from which the participants had no choice but to fall back in line with the society at large for the sake of mere survival.

The Problem

Migratory movement of a voluntary nature acquired prominence in the wake of economic development ushered in with the Industrial Revolution of 18th century. Since then, movements of people in search of better economic prospects/employment opportunities gained momentum in various parts of the world. Side by side, a shift of population from the rural areas in the countryside to urban centres where factories were opened, leading to an urban growth ensued. In England where the Industrial Revolution had its beginnings, the urban population which formed hardly 23 per cent in 1801 increased to 32 per cent by 1851. As Redford puts, "In England a great part of the growth of town population during the half-century had been due to the mushroom growth of industrial centres".[1] Another pattern which acquired worldwide significance was the large scale migration of Europeans to the new world, known as transatlantic migration. According to an estimate made by an authority nearly 36 million aliens of European origin reached the U.S.A. between 1820 and

1924.[2] During the initial stages, the overwhelming majority of the migrants were from the central parts of Europe but subsequently migrants from all other parts of Europe also joined the stream. They abandoned their traditional callings in the agricultural sector and ended up as factory hands. The complexion of the migrants and the pattern and direction of migration underwent changes in course of time.

While the migratory movements of such gigantic proportions were underway in Europe, Indian sub-continent also witnessed the emergence of altogether different patterns of migration. Migrations of labour to the plantations in the tropical countries under "the indenture" and "kangani" systems were the patterns which originated in the Indian soil from the earlier decades of nineteenth century.[3] Migrants under these patterns were unskilled agricultural workers recruited for the purpose of working in the tropical plantations. The Caribbean islands, Guiana, Natal, East Africa, Mauritius, Sri Lanka, Malaysia and Fiji were the important destinations of the migrants sent under those systems. Migrants were recruited mainly from Eastern U.P., Bihar, Orissa, and the Tamil and Telugu districts of the erstwhile Madras presidency. Since the migrants under these systems were recruited and sent to the foreign lands under state patronage, the systems were known as assisted labour migration. New patterns like the trader migration, professional migration, and settler migration also emerged subsequently. Proportionately, more number of migrants hailed from Punjab and Gujarat under the new patterns. A large number of migrants from India opted to settle down in the places of destination. It is estimated that as many as 2.79 million persons born in India or of Indian extraction were found to be living in foreign lands as on 1921.[4]

Close on the heels of emigration to foreign lands, different patterns of internal migration also originated in India. An important pattern was the migration of workers to the newly opened plantations in Assam and South India. Migration also took place to the newly opened factories at Bombay and Calcutta. In close succession, traders and professionals also began to set on a migratory movement. An interesting case of trader migration was that of the Marwaris whose migratory movement from their native places in Rajastan had in fact its origin much before the British occupation of India. The number of Marwaris living in different parts of India like Assam, Calcutta, Bombay, Hyderabad etc. was stated to be anywhere between 40,000 – 50,000 in 1911.[5]

The intensity of the migratory movement has not been uniform throughout India. The important centres of origin of the migrants were the regions like Punjab, Eastern U.P., Bihar, Orissa, Tamil and Telugu districts of the erstwhile Madras presidency. There was practically no migration from regions like Bengal, Maharashtra, Madhya Pradesh, Kerala etc. during the initial stages. However, migrants also began to move out from some of these non-migratory regions in course of time. The present Kerala, the Malayalam speaking state in India, which then consisted of the princely state of Travancore in the south, the princely state of Cochin the middle and the British administered Malabar district in the north, is one of such regions, whose sons also started to move in different directions.

Though Kerala has emerged as an important migrating state during recent years, very few Keralites seemed to have moved out of Kerala till the end of 19th century. Instead, Kerala had been a haven of inmigrants like the Konkanis, Pattar Brahmins, the Rowther Muslims etc. from the neighbouring states. Even trading communities like the Gujaratis, Sindhis and Chettis had their ethnic enclaves in the commercial centres of Kerala. Furthermore, when the Europeans opened plantations of coffee and tea in the Travancore region of Kerala during the latter half of the 19th century, the bulk of the labour supply came from the then Madras presidency.[6] Not surprisingly, the census reports of the closing decades of 19th century speak of Keralites as a home-bound people apparently because of the absence of any settlement of Keralites in other parts of India, though Kerala was well connected even with foreign lands from ancient past.[7]

However, the Keralites who were reluctant to move out of their moorings transformed themselves into a highly mobile class in India since the turn of the century. The migratory movement which started in trickles acquired the characteristics of a stream after the end of the First World War. The census report of 1921 of the princely state of Travancore describes the change in the attitude towards migration thus:

"If facilities are given for slightly higher remuneration than those obtained in India, persons are prepared to go abroad without allowing religion, caste or sex to stand in their way is evident from the number of persons who have gone from this state to Mesopotamia".[8] Since then, there were ups and downs in the migratory flow on account of the international developments like the Depression of the thirties, the Second World War, liquidation of colonialism etc. Nevertheless, the sons of Kerala continued to move in large numbers to countries like Sri Lanka, Burma, Malaysia, Saudi Arabia, Kuwait, United Arab Emirates etc. and to various places within the country like Mumbai, Chennai, Bangalore, Delhi etc.

How Kerala could emerge as a strong migrating region in India since the dawn of the twentieth century is a question which calls for deeper probing. The question acquires added significance because Kerala could overtake many other leading emigrating regions like Tamil Nadu,

Gujarat, Orissa, Andhra Pradesh in the intensity of migration within a short period of time. Once started the process seemed to have taken new patterns and acquired larger dimensions. The manner in which the process has acquired new patterns over the years is also an equally important question requiring exploration.

Studies on migration are galore in India. However, almost all of them focus from the all India angle. Similarly, studies on migration from a historical angle are scanty. Even when historical aspects are uncovered, the focus is very often on the consequences and not on the causes of migration. According to an author, causes have been very often given only perfunctory attention.[9] At the same time, migration from Kerala, especially from a historical angle has received scant attention in any of the studies, though migrants from Kerala constitute a conspicuous section during recent years. In his study, "Migration and Economic Development of Kerala", Joseph focuses on peasant migrants from Travancore region to Malabar region of Kerala only and not to other parts of India.[10]

The present study aims at unravelling the pattern, direction and magnitude of migration from Kerala to foreign lands and to other parts of India and also to trace the various factors and events which prompted the migratory flow from a historical angle. The study focuses on various stages of migratory movement ushered in during 20th century. Such a time period is chosen because migration from Kerala became a conspicuous phenomenon only since the turn of 20th century. At the same time, migration with a colonial heritage came to an end by 1960 and almost all the colonies to which migrants moved from India became independent by that time. Furthermore, most of the countries revised their policies towards immigration since the sixties. Within India, reorganisation of states on linguistic lines took place in1956, and Kerala became a unified state only on that date. With the launching of planning an era of industrial development ushered in India. As a result of all those developments, patterns of migration and the magnitude of migration would have certainly undergone serious changes during 20th century in Kerala.

Methodology

Historical processes as such are moulded and conditioned by various economic, demographic, political, social and cultural factors. Migration on its part as Berliner puts, "rarely occurs in pure forms in nature, but always in connection with other social processes".[11] Naturally, the study would explore how those various factors have influenced and conditioned the migratory process over the years. At the same time migratory movements are influenced by past events. As Timothy Halton concurs, "Persistence is likely to matter in accounting for the variety in European emigration experiences in the late 19th century. Historical events like famines and revolutions are likely to have potent influence on emigration experiences even after the events have disappeared from the memory of current generation. Low French emigration in the 1890s may have its source in the revolution induced land reforms a century before and high Irish emigration in 1890s may have its source to the famine half a century ago".[12] The study would naturally probe into those past events, like the land reforms etc. which would have shaped the pattern of migration at a later date in Kerala. The study would be seeking the process of migration from Kerala within the context of migration in India as a whole. Historical analogy of carefully selected events in other parts of India and elsewhere would be compared and contrasted with the developments in Kerala.

Malayalees form approximately 95 per cent of the population of Kerala. Apparently, all the migrants will not be Malayalees. Nevertheless, the study very often makes use of the term "Malayalee" in the place of Keralite, apparently for projecting the linguistic identity of the migrants as well as for the exigencies of comparable data; though the two terms are not conceptually the same. Census reports over the years would the important source of data. Such of those records and documents which we can lay hands on including those available in the archives at Delhi and Chennai constitute another source of data. Newspaper reports and other publications will be another source.

Scheme of the Study

In the light of what is stated above, the study would be on the following lines. Chapter 2 will be dealing with the questions why was migratory movement absent from Kerala for a long period and how could migratory movement acquire the status of a stream during the years following the First World War. Chapter 3 deals with migration of Keralites to foreign lands. Trends in the internal migration over the years upto the end of the 20th century form the theme of Chapter 4. The focus of Chapter 5 will be on the profile of the migrants from different parts of India. A comparison of the profile of the migrants from Kerala with those from other parts of India will also be attempted in Chapter 5. A significant section of the migrants from Kerala would have opted to settle down in various parts of India. A brief account of the settlement process along with the patterns of settlements would be delineated in Chapter 6. Chapter 7 will provide the summary and conclusion of the study.

Notes and References

1. Redford, Arthur: *Labour Migration in England (1800-1850)* (Manchester, Manchester University Press, 1926) p. 6.
2. It is estimated that nearly 50 million people moved into the continents of North and South America from the rest of the world between 1846 and 1924. The U.S. alone received 36 million foreigners of whom nearly 90 per cent were from Europe. See Brinley, Thomas, *International Migration and Economic Development: A Trend Report and Bibliography* (Paris, Unesco 1961), p. 9.
3. The "indenture" system was originally a method under which Chinese workers were recruited to the plantations in South America and Cuba from the Portuguese Colony of Macao. When slavery was abolished in the British empire in 1834 the indenture system was adopted for importing labour mainly from India to the plantations in the Tropical colonies. The migrant labourers under the indenture system were bound by a contract to serve in the plantations for a few years, under terms and conditions which were in no way better than slavery. Recruitment of labour under indenture was stopped temporarily in 1916 under the Defence of India Act. The system was finally abolished in 1920 as a result of strong public opposition against it in India. A slightly modified version of the same known as kangani system was adopted for the purpose of labour migration to Malaysia and Sri Lanka (see Kingsley Davis, *Population of India and Pakistan* (Princeton University, New Jersey 1951, pp. 102-104). See also N.Gangulee, *Indians in Empire Overseas: A Survey* (London, The New India Publishing House, 1951).
4. Findlay Shirras: "Indian Migration" in Willcox, Walter (ed.): *International Migration: Vol.II Interpretation* (New York, Gorden Reach Publication, 1969), p. 592.
5. Timberg Thomas A: *The Marwaris: From Traders to Industrialists* (New Delhi, Vikas Publishing House, 1978), p. 110.
6. The number of coolies employed in the estates in Travancore totalled 14497 in 1896. Out of them (1) imported labour from the former Madras Presidency formed 60 per cent; (2) Imported labour from Mysore formed 20 per cent; and (3) Local labour formed 20 per cent. See Report of the *South Indian Planters Enquiry Committee 1896* (Madras, Government Press).
7. The Census Report of Madras presidency for the year 1901 contains the follwing significant observation about the mentality of the people of Malabar towards migration: "Cut off as it is by the hills from the rest of the Presidency, immigrants to it are rare and the people are stay at home-folk", See Census Report of Madras 1901, Vol. I, Report (Madras, Government Press).
8. GOT, *Census of India 1921, Travancore*, Part I (Trivandrum, Superintendent, Govt. Press), p. 28.
9. Timothy J. Hatton (1998) in *The Age of Mass Migration Causes and*

Economic Impact (Oxford University Press, p. 5) quotes from Thistlethwaite F. *Migration from Europe Overseas in the Nineteenth and Twentieth Centuries* reprinted in R J Vecoli and Som Snike (ed.) *A Century of European Migration 1830-1900* (Urban University Press, Illinois Press 1991), pp. 19-20.

10. Joseph, K.V., *Migration and Economic Development of Kerala* (Delhi, Mittal Publications, 1988).
11. Berliner, Joseph, S. "International Migration: A Comparative Disciplinary View" in Brown Alan Neuberger Edgon (ed.): *Internal Migration: A Comparative Perspective* (New York, Academic Press, 1977), p. 446.
12. Hatton, Timothy, J. and Williamson, Jeffrey: *The Age of Mass Migration Causes and Economic Impact* (New York, Oxford University Press, 1998), p. 14.

Chapter 2

Beginnings of the Process of Migration

In the previous chapter, we have seen that there was practically no migration from Kerala till towards the end of nineteenth century. Moreover, the migratory movement which started in trickles from Kerala since the turn of the century acquired the characteristics of a stream during the years following the First World War. In this context, the questions is, why has migratory movement been absent from Kerala till towards the end of nineteenth century. The question assumes added significance because Kerala had maritime trade connections with foreign countries dating back to the ancient past. Merchants and sailors from ancient Rome, Palestine, Arabia, Persia, China etc., used to frequent Kerala coast and quite a few of them settled down in Kerala. Furthermore, Kerala was in regular contact with the Europeans since the arrival of Vasco da Gama in Kozhikode in 1498. Interestingly, Joseph, 'the Indian' a native of Cranganore in Kerala accompanied Cabral to Lisbon in 1501 and visited many European countries.[1] Since then, Keralalites used to visit various parts of Europe and West Asia for one reason or other. Nevertheless, nobody opted to migrate from Kerala. In this context, why Keralites remained as an immobile class, is a question requiring serious consideration. Another important question is, how could an immobile community transform themselves into a mobile class during the years following the First World War?

The answer to these questions would be sought within the context of the migratory movement from the country as a whole. An elucidation of various theoretical formulations on migration would be useful for probing the question from different angles.

Approaches to the Study on Migration

Though migratory movements have acquired new dimensions since 18th century, very few theoretical formulations have been evolved for a long period. The classical economists who dominated the intellectual realm for a long period did not think of formulating any theory on migration. What they did was to advocate free trade and competition of the laissez-faire mould in the place of utility of poverty advocated by the mercantalists. Internal mobility of factors of production as a concomitant to competition was the only option which they could think of as an analytical concept on migration. Nevertheless, some of them advocated colonialism as an antidote to the law of diminishing returns.

The pioneer who provided a theoretical framework was Ravenstein. According to him, migration between two places will invariably be related to distance and migrants move in stages from distant lands. The movement is to the centres of commerce and trade which accelerates over time as a result of the increase in the means of locomotion. The propensity to migrate would be more with the inhabitants of the rural rather than with those of the urban areas. Migrants are motivated by the human desire to better themselves in material respects.[2] However, Ravenstein's laws are mere generalisations which do not encompass any theoretical formulation.

Since then, many scholars have introduced different formulations to uncover various aspects of migration. The dominant approach is to regard migration as an equilibrating process arising from the interaction of push and pull factors. Different authors have put forward their own versions of the equilibrating process. The most important among them is the one introduced by Lee. His approach is to explain migration in terms of a set of factors at origin and destination, a set of intervening obstacles and a series of personal factors. In any area there are countless forces which act to hold people in that area or attract people to it and there are others which tend to repel them. People are indifferent to some others. The effect of these forces varies from person to person depending on his age, experience, education, skill etc. He also introduced the concept of intervening obstacles like distance, cost of transport, restrictive immigration laws etc. which also exert varying levels of influence on migration.[3] Therefore what he concedes is that the actual decision to migrate is never conceptually rational. The volume of migration depends on the degree of diversity of the area, occupation and size of the population. Migration tends to increase with time and state of progress of the society. However, his variables are not suitable for quantification, because like Bentham's calculus of pleasure and pain, the calculus of +S and -S at origin and destination is always inexact. Another important problem in any study on migration is to identify how the plus and minus points pave the way for the emergence of migration.

Another formulation links migration with development. Authors like John Fei, Arthur Lewis, Gustav and at a later date Todaro are associated with the model. Under the model, the economy consists of rural subsistence sector and modern urban sector. What happens is the transfer of surplus labour from the rural sector to the expanding urban sector which is susceptible to capitalist development.[4] The theory is applicable only to the migration of labour from the rural sector to the urban sector in which jobs carrying higher rates of wages would be available.

Migration is regarded as an activity involving the calculation of costs and returns. Larry S. Sjaastad, the exponent of the theory regards migration as a resource allocating endeavour in which calculations of costs and returns are of primary importance. Both the monetary and non-monetary elements are included under the rubrics of costs. Non-monetary costs include psychic costs also.[5] Nevertheless, when it comes to the actual calculation, only money costs are taken into account excluding non-money cost. However, the historical context under which each pattern of migration originates and the manner in which the urge for migration grows in the minds of only a few selected groups cannot be explained in terms of costs and returns.

Migration occurs when place utility is higher in a new location than in the present location according to Wolpert. Place utility represents the social, economic and other costs and benefits derived from an individual's integration at some position in some space. The range of alternatives will be limited by one's own experience, information available and even position in his life cycle. It is known as situational approach because the determinants of migration like population density, political and social structure etc. vary from situation to situation.[6] How the situation varies from place to place and the method through which it changes are more important in determining the type and the size of migration.

The aforesaid approaches focus on individual decision making as the primary concern in any study on migration. The individual decision making is influenced by the social, economic and political conditions under which an individual acts and makes a living. Naturally, any study on migration without taking cognizance of the wider socio-economic matrix becomes only a partial approach. These approaches regard migration as an equilibrating process in which labour moves from a place with low productivity to another with high productivity. Actually, any pattern of migration is a particular historical event relevant to that period only. The equilibrium approach is insensitive to the causes of population movements that are specific to particular historical periods.

In view of the inadequacy of the different versions of equilibrium approach to uncover the process of migration especially from the historical angle, an alternative formulation known as historical structural perspective, has been introduced by some other scholars. Those associated with the approach include Portes, Cardoz, Balan, Mangalam etc. According to their line of thinking any study on migration must necessarily probe into the pressures and counter-pressures both internal and external to the economy which cause changes in the organisation of production. It is the historical processes which determine the availability of labour and effect changes in the migration patterns. The structural transformation of social set up rather than individual motives assumes priority in any migration stream. Migration becomes a class phenomenon where the unit of analysis should be the stream rather than the individual components. Any study on migration therefore calls for a broader theory of socio-economic and political changes in which migration constitutes a part.[7]

According to Zelinsky, personal mobility through time and space constitutes an essential component of modernization process. The mobility transition of a society corresponds to the demographic transition. There are five stages in the demographic transition. No migration is feasible during phase I which corresponds to pre-modern society. During phase II, representing early transitional society, various patterns of migration takes place. Migration slackens during phase III. Immigration of unskilled workers on a limited scale is feasible from underdeveloped areas during phase IV. There will be no migration during phase V. The emphasis is on phase II in which different types of migration as happened during the nineteenth century England, and as is heppening at present in the newly developed countries of Asia are relevant.[8] However, the analysis is insufficient to explain why and how different patterns of migration have taken place. It is also doubtful whether the same mobility pattern holds good throughout the world.

Notwithstanding the significance of the parameters inherent with the "historical structural perspective" or the "mobility transition" in unravelling the migratory movements from a historical angle, none of them by itself is sufficient to explain the different aspects of migration. The individual motivations are as important as changes in the structural formation in promoting migration. Similarly, the role of pioneering migrants in promoting new waves of migration is also a well-recognised fact. In brief, as Prejor puts, "no existing model theories or concepts can be transformed directly from one field of migration studies to another".[9]

Naturally an eclectic approach, incorporating elements from different disciplines as well as divergent formulations and approaches will be adopted for the present study. Such an approach becomes inevitable because as stated in Chapter 1, migration occurs " in connection with other social processes"[10]. Other social processes include the wider social, cultural, economic, demographic and political changes as well as the historical process of development. As Rao puts it, "any study of migration should consider the historical development of the region, the wider economic and political conditions which regulate and condition the nature of employment opportunities".[11] What is attempted in the study is to proceed from the wider socio-economic and cultural evolution of India from a historical angle for the purpose of uncovering the migratory movement over the years.

Constraints to Migration

As already stated, migratory movements do not erupt all on a sudden. Certain favourable conditions encompassing economic, social and political factors should emerge as pre-conditions for migratory process to commence. Prior to the Industrial Revolution, the social, economic, political and even legal systems were operating in such a way as to prevent any migratory movement in the European countries like Great Britain, France, Prussia etc. Only with the growth of modern industries, people from the countryside began to move to the localities where factories were opened.

The conditions in India were totally unfavourable and even opposed to any migratory movement. The economic system with the cultivation of land for the production of subsistence food materials as the main productive activity was primitive by all standards. Normally under subsistence system all sections of the cultivating classes would be rooted in the ancestral soil with great apathy for spatial and occupational mobility. The bulk of the people would be content with meeting the bare needs of life. The conditions in India with the self-sufficient subsistence village economies at the grass-root level, which maintained very little contact with the market or outside world, were still more precarious. Radha Kamal Mukerjee describes the conditions which prevailed in the Indian villages during the greater part of 19th century with the following words:

> "The village is still almost self-sufficing and is itself an economic unit. The village agriculturists grow all the food necessary for the inhabitants of the village. The smith makes the ploughshare of the cultivator and the few iron utensils required for the household. He supplies these to the people but does not get any money in return. He is recompensated by mutual services from his fellow villagers.

The porter supports him with pots and the weaver with cloth and oil man with oil. From the cultivator each of these artisans receives his traditional share of grain. Thus almost all the economic transactions are carried on without the use of money".[12]

The conditions in Kerala were still more rigid during the nineteenth century. The bulk of the people led a very frugal life with very little contact with outside world. Ward and Conner who made a systematic survey in Travancore and Cochin regions of Kerala during the early decades of 19th century made the following observation regarding the conditions then prevailing in Travancore. "..... although it must be observed that the desires and wants of the people are still more limited than those of other natives and with very few exceptions they supply themselves from their own sources, they have but little inclination to imitate our manners nor a taste aggreable to our productions".[13]

The items for which the Keralites depended on the market were cloth, salt and tobacco. These items were consumed at the barest minimum level. Even during the beginning of the twentieth century the want of an average peasant was very few as to be inferred from the following observation made by another authority: "His wants are few, rice *conjee* is the chief diet and for the rest esculent roots with which the country abounds, supply the deficient sustenance, his clothing is scanty, jewels are nearly unknown ..."[14]

Notwithstanding the constraints migratory movements were taking place on a fairly large scale from different parts of India for one reason or other. One of the most important reasons was the frequent failure of the monsoon which resulted in droughts and famines in various parts of India. Such calamities used to result in large scale migration. On the other hand, Kerala was free from such natural calamities. Instances of famine were unheard of thanks to the bountiful climatic conditions. Even when Travancore region became deficient in so far as rice production is concerned towards the close of nineteenth century, the deficit could be covered by cultivating tapioica, a tuber crop imported from South America. Needless to say, the need for compulsory migration was totally nil in Kerala in sharp contrast to the rest of India.

In India as a whole and Kerala in particular, the deep-rooted caste structure has acted as another constraint to migration. The stratification of the society based on caste system with the imperative of religious sanctions behind it severally restricted the scope for migration in the normal course. The stigma of pollution attached to the inferior castes operated as a permanent handicap to the members belonging to such communities to move around or to migrate. The lower castes were even denied the right to travel through the highways because of the pollution attached to them. In Kerala, untouchability was carried to the grotesque lengths with differential distances of polluting contacts defined for each caste; in the most extreme cases to shouting distances. Shea sums up the net effect thus: "A low caste person outside his village could if he were a Hindu pursue no occupation; within his village he was restricted to work spurned by the higher castes".[15]

Absence of population pressure was another constraint on migration particularly from Kerala. The population of Kerala was only 65 lakhs towards the close of nineteenth century and no population pressure was experienced in the region. In fact, the Census Commissioner of Travancore had made the following suggestion in 1891. He stated, "whatever may be the effect of the pressure of population some generations hence, there is at present a good field of work. I mean the work by the hand for the Madras ryot, especially of the congested districts, in the Travancore hills and jungle valleys".[16]

Further, Kerala is a narrow strip of land sandwitched between the Western Ghats and Arabian sea. Smooth passage to the rest of the country is impeded by the long stretch of steep mountains from north to south. Within the region, the mountains, valleys, hills and waterlogged paddylands intermingled with each other in such a way as to hinder smooth movements. Further, the innumerable rivers cutting across the region from east to west render mobility within Kerala still more difficult. The settlement pattern also makes migration a very difficult process. Unlike the clustered houses in each village, the houses are scattered and spread out throughout the region with very little contact with one another. Though Kerala has a lengthy coastline, there is no evidence of Keralites having moved to distant lands by taking advantage of the opening to the sea in the past.

Partly as a result of the peculiar geographical conditions, Kerala was divided into small principalities independent of each other with no central or unified authority particularly throughout history in the past. At the close of eighteenth century, Kerala came under the control of the Britishers. Malabar, the northern part comprising nearly 40 per cent of the land area of Kerala was brought directly under the British administration as a district of the old Madras presidency. The princely state of Travancore comprising the southern part and the princely state of Cochin, occupying the middle of Kerala, continued to remain as self-governing states under British suzeranity. Since these states remained as separate entities within the British Indian Empire, the citizens of these states also opted by and large to confine themselves within the limits of the respective state boundaries. Naturally, migratory movement from the princely states was absent for all practical purposes, though the citizens of the princely states were also entitled to travel or settle down in any part of India.

Notwithstanding the retarding effect of the constraints, Indian sub-continent began to display migratory movement right from the early decades of nineteenth century. In 1834-35, the year from which continuous data is available, as many as 62000 persons left India for different parts of the world. Out of them 52000 persons returned to India leaving a net migration of 10000 persons. The number went on increasing and during the period 1896-1900, the number of migrants totalled 1962000 as against 694000 return migration.[17] The question is, how such large scale migration could take place at a time when none of the conditions then prevailing in India were conducive to any migration at all.

The migratory movement of the nineteenth century was mainly to the Caribbean islands, Guiana, Mauritius, Natal, Sri Lanka, Malaysia, Burma, Fiji; all of them falling within the category of British colonies. The migrants consisted mostly of coolie labourers meant to work in the sugar, coffee and tea plantations. The pull factors for such migration arose from the constellation of certain developments. The European powers established their colonial empire for the purpose of exploiting the colonies and thereby enriching themselves. The citizens of the European nations which established the colonies opened plantations of sugar, coffee and tea in the colonies. The labour requirements of the plantations were met by engaging slaves as labourers. However, when slavery was abolished in the British Empire in 1831, the planters found it difficult to secure the services of enough labour as the ex-slaves refused to work in the plantations. Their attempts to secure labour from other sources were not at all successful. When their attempts failed to secure enough labourers, their attention turned towards India as a potential source for recruiting labour. Accordingly, they approached the Government of India for recruiting labour from India. The government on its part was too eager to help the planters and issued necessary permission for the recruitment of labour from India. No sooner had the government gave permission for the recruitment, the planters started to recruit labour and take them to the plantations located in distant lands like Mauritius, Guiana, Trinidad, Fiji etc. The mode of recruitment and emigration of labour, as stated in Chapter I, was under indenture system.[18]

When the pull factors of such a nature emerged, push factors for the movement were equally strong. W.Crooke, graphically describes the miserable conditions which prevailed in most parts of north India during eighteenth century and which prompted the movement of people thus: "The castes which live by unskilled labour are in wretched conditions, ill-fed, ill-clothed with no resources to withstand the failure of the monsoon and the scarcity more or less severe which attend to such a calamity".[19] In fact, the appearance of famines one after another in succession in 1770, 1784, 1804, 1837, 1877, 1878 and 1892 in Bengal and northern part of India which accelerated the misery of the people provided the immediate promptings for migration.[20] Further, the taxation system was so severe that many of the tenants were always in debt. The land tenure system actually deprived the peasants of their right over land. Such deplorable conditions made the recruitment of labour for emigration to the plantations, a smooth affair. Kondapi explains the whole process in graphic terms thus:

"It was in such a predicament that the planters from foreign countries approached the Indian government for a steady and continuous supply of Indian labour. The earnest entreaties and the rosy promises held out by the colonial planters and government at a most psychological hour proved decisive. And organised emigration of Indian labour to the British colonies began from Bengal in 1838 under the supervision and direction of the government of India. The active sympathy of the government of India accelerated the pace of migration. The colonial government appointed professional recruiters who visited Indian villages stricken with crop failure, or pilgrim centres during days of high religious congregations and entrapped poor Indians by dangling before them hopeful pictures of prospects in the colonies. They fulfilled the legal formalities with official connivance of the recruiting depots and took them over for indentured service".[21]

Hundreds of thousands of persons from India moved to different parts of the world over the years when indenture system was in vogue. Many of them returned to India. However, some of them opted to settle down in the countries of destination. The number of immigrants in various countries from India under indenture system has been as given in Table 2.1.

As a result of the massive flow of immigrants from India leading to the settlement of a good many among them in the countries of destination, the people of Indian origin increased to more than three fourth of the total population of Mauritius. Though Indians formed the majority or near majority in countries like Fiji and Guiana, they were

Table 2.1: Volume of Indian Immigrants Under Indenture System

Country	*Periods*	*No. of Indian Immigrants*
Mauritius	1834-1912	453063
British Guiana	1838-1817	238909
South Africa	1860-1911	152184
Trinidad	1845-1917	143939
Reunion	1829-1924	118000
Fiji	1879-1916	60969
Guadelope	1854-1885	42326
East Africa (Kenya/Uganda)	1895-1901	39771
Jamaica	1845-1885	36420
Surinam (Dutch)	1873-1916	34000
Martinique	1854-1889	25509
Seychelles	1899-1916	6319
St Lucia	1858-1895	4350
Grenada	1865-1885	320
St.Vincent	1861-1880	2472

Source: Clarke, Peach and Vertovec, *South Asians, Overseas* Ch. 9. Quoted by Ceri Peach, "Three Phases of South Asian Emigrration" in Judith Brown(ed), *Migration: The Asian Experience* (Oxford, St. Martin's, 1994, p. 4).

denied political power. Migration under indenture was stopped around 1920, as the system was full of abuses and malpractices. Since then, free labour migration became the accepted pattern.

While migration under indenture system was in force migrants also moved to countries like Malaysia, Sri Lanka and Burma under slightly different system. Most of the migrants moved to those neighbouring countries under what is known as *Kangani* system. Under *Kangani* system, the *Kangani*, usually a labourer already in employment as a labourer on the plantations recruited labourers, very often his relatives or neighbours The actual number of migrants to Malaysia, Sri Lanka and Burma was much more than under the indenture system.

Tardy Origin of Migration from Kerala

Most of the migrants under indenture system hailed from eastern parts of U.P., Bihar and Orissa. Migrants under *Kangani* system hailed mainly from Tamil and Telugu districts of the Madras presidency. Both were state aided migrations. The planters on their part had sent agents to different parts of India for recruiting and despatching migrants from India. The planters did not fail to send professional agents to Kerala and recruiting centres were opened in two centres, viz., Palghat and

Tirur in Kerala.[22] In close succession, a few *cherumas* and other slaves of the soil seemed to have emigrated from Malabar for the purpose of seeking freedom from a life of "incessant toil and shameful expoloitation" by the landlords.[23] However, they could recruit very few people and migration was scanty if not nil from Malabar region. According to the census report of 1901, the number of persons who migrated to different places were: (1) Mauritius 22; (2) Burma (64); Ceylon 247 and Malaya nil.[24]

Other evidences also point that migration from Kerala was only on a negligible scale even during the beginning of the twentieth century. Out of a total number of 294919 migrants returned from different countries to the Madras presidency, only 1283 were to Malabar district in 1908. The actual number of migrants shipped to Fiji from Malabar was only 43 out of a total of 874 from the Presidency in 1906. Similarly, the number was only 24 out of 47787 to Ceylon in 1906. No separate figures are available in respect of the number of migrants to Malaya.[25] While migration, though on a negligible scale took place from Mabalar, there was practically no migration either from Travancore or Cochin states as to be inferred from proceedings No.34 dated 3rd July 1903 of the Government of Madras wherein it is stated that "emigration from either of these two states appears to be of rare occurrence".[26]

Another important destination of emigrants was Burma, which was part of India till 1935. Since the annexation of Burma by the Britishers, streams of migrants began to move from various parts of India. However, migration from Kerala was only negligible if not nil. The total Malayalam speaking people in Burma numbered 324 in 1901.[27] On the other hand, there were as many as 130,000 Indians in Rangoon, the Capital City of Burma alone in 1901.

The European entrepreneurs also opened plantations of tea, coffee and rubber in Assam and South India on similar pattern they opened plantations in the other tropical colonies. These planations also called the service of large number of workers. Local labour was not available in sufficient numbers. Naturally they had to recruit labourers from other parts of India. Jha explains the situation thus:

> "The colonial government knew that the meek and docile tribals of Chotanagpur and the plains of Bihar and United Provinces have proved very successful in the sugar plantations of Mauritius and West Indies. Therefore they started importing labourers to North East from the same scene".[28]

A system akin to indenture known as "maistry system" was

introduced for this purpose. Hundreds and thousands of people from those areas migrated to the plantations. The number of migrants employed in the plantations under *maistry* system in 1874-75 for example was 44454.[29] Available evidences point to the absence of migration from Kerala to the tea gardens of Assam.

Though large scale emigration involving millions of people took place from the Indian sub-continent during the nineteenth century, emigration from Kerala region during that period was nominal. The migratory movement from the Indian sub-continent was a state patronised activity of assisted labour migration which was in no way different from slavery. In the words of Kingsley Davis, "The only comparable situation was that of the Africans crossing the Atlantic under the aegis of slavery whereas the Indian migration was a substitute, for that condition".[30] Such a situation with full scope for exploitation could emerge in India because of the abject poverty of the masses. Frequent natural calamities contributed further to the misery of the people. As Kondapi has pointed out, the frequency of migration was actually higher during years of distress.[31] In Kerala on the other hand, the bountiful agro-climatic conditions prevented the emergence of such a deplorable situation. The Statistical Atlas of the Malabar district for the year 1905 contains a significant observation which corroborates the same in clear terms. The observation is, "there is no doubt that the general standard of living in Malabar is much higher than in majority of other districts east of the ghats".[32] Apparently, the attempts of the recruiters could not succeed, so long as the plight of the ordinary people was not so miserable. The settlement pattern in Kerala was another factor which could frustrate the attempts of the recruiters.

New Patterns of Migration

The era of economic/employment oriented modern migratory movement ushered in with the disappearance of the age old mode of life resulting from the changes in the organisation of agriculture and industry. The old order came to an end with the Industrial Revolution. The transatlantic migration of the Europeans could ensue only when changes of far reaching nature had occured in Europe with the Industrial Revolution. Handlin describes in graphic terms the epoch making changes which paved the way for large scale migration of European peasants during nineteenth century thus:

"For centuries the size of the population, the amount of available land, the quantity of productive surplus and the pressure of family stability achieved together a steady balance that preserved the village way of life. Only slowly in a few places were there signs of unsteadiness in the seventeenth century; then more distinctly and in more places in the eighteenth century. After 1800, the elements of the old equilibrium disintegrated. The old social structure tottered; gathering momentum from its own fall; it was unable to right itself and under the impact of successive shocks collapsed. Then the peasants could no longer hang on; when even to stay meant to change, they had to leave".[33]

The Indian sub-continent also would have witnessed changes somewhat similar in nature before the beginning of any migration of a voluntary nature in contrast to what happened when the state sponsored indenture migration of labour was in the offing. In the place of the wantlessness of the past, marked changes became visible in the attitude of the people towards material culture, style of life and mode of eocnomic activities towards the closing decades of nineteenth century. Migratory movement of a voluntary nature to those places where opportunities for better economic prospects were available ensued in close succession as a concomitant to those developments. The following words from Radha Kamal Mukherjee illustrate the whole process in clear terms:

> "New economic ideas have now begun to influence the minds of the villagers. In some of the villages, the weavers and blacksmiths have no doubt been compelled to leave their occupations on account of foreign competition, but more are leaving their hereditary occupations of their own accord. Not only the middle class but the field labourers have also found their ancestral occupations not sufficiently paying and have felt the need of moving to other places. The government public works, the factories, the tea, indigo and coffee plantations, the mining operations as well as the facilities for foreign migration also tend to shake the old immobility of labour".[34]

New patterns of migration also emerged with those developments. As already stated, the pattern which was dominant in the past was the state assisted labour migration. As a result, emigration from India was identified as coolie migration which brought only discredit to the country. Instead, free migration; the new pattern emerged with the changes in the socio-economic formation. Under free migration, streams of migrants began to move to Sri Lanka, South Africa, East Africa and Malaya. Nevertheless, majority of them were agricultural labourers. Another pattern was also in the offing. It was the migration of semi-skilled workers who reached East African colonies. It was these workers from India who constructed railways in the East African region.

Close on the heels of unassisted labour migration, traders consisting of businessmen, petty contractors, moneylenders, shop-keepers and hawkers emigrated to various countries, where Indians had migrated earlier. They were free-migrants by all standards who moved with their own resources usually with bits of capital, and sufficient experience in those kinds of trade they sought to practice.[35] This category consisted of Chettiars from Tamil Nadu, Marwaris from Rajasthan, Banias from U.P., Jains from Gujarat and Parsis from Bombay. This new class of migrants contributed much to the development of those places where they set had foot. The contributions of Indians to the development of East Africa was a well-known fact and in appreciation of the same; Winston Churchill paid growing tribute to them with the following words: "It was the Sikh soldier who borne the honourable part in the conquest of these East African countries. It is the Indian trader who penetrating and maintaining himself in all sorts of places to which no White man would go or in which no White man could earn a living, has more than any one else developed the early beginnings of trade and opened up the first slender means of communication".[36]

The educated class whose number began to swell also resorted to a migratory process to those places were Indians had gone earlier. At the same time, the demand for educated persons to handle middle ranking occupations were also going up. In the words of Kingsley Davis, "these were far less important numerically than the labourers; but they raised different problems and acquired political significance far beyond their numbers".[37] These new classes of migrants could thus erase to some extent the discredit created by the earlier coolie migrants in foreign lands.

Significantly, the beginnings of Indian migration to North America were made during this period. The laws then prevailing in the USA as well as the public opinion were opposed to any migration from India. Indians were not eligible to become citizens of the USA on those days. In fact, one official committee indicated the Indians as the least desirable race admitted to the U.S. Nevertheless, a few Indians managed to reach the USA with great difficulty. Even then the actual number of Indians in the USA totalled 5811 by 1911. Canadian laws as well as the law enforcing authority, the police were equally unfriendly to the immigrants from India. Nevertheless, nearly 5000 Indians managed to reach Canada by the end of 19th century. Almost all the immigrants from India to the U.S. and Canada were from the Punjab with the Sikhs forming the largest group. Most of the Indians congregated to the west coast of the U.S.A. and Canada. [38] Some Parsi students and businessmen also managed to reach the U.S. towards the close of 19th century.

Migration to Great Britain till towards the close of 19th century was a rare event though India was bound with Great Britain for more than a century. Most of those who managed to migrate were students and businessmen with the Parsis forming the pioneering group. Interestingly, three Parsi gentlemen, viz., Dadabhai Naoroji, M.M. Bhownagree and Saklatvala had the rare distinction of becoming members of British Parliament during the formative days of migration to Great Britain.[39]

Migratory movement also started within the country also. The newly opened factories at Bombay and Calcutta began to attract different categories of workers. Actually, when mills were opened during the later half of nineteenth century, enough workers were not coming forward to take up employment. In the words of Gunnar Myrdal, "The nascent textile industry in India had to struggle a persistent scarcity of labour throughout a period of rapid growth upto the First World War and beyond".[40] In the absence of enough workers, village menials and pauperised peasants became the main source of labour supply.

Beginnings of the Process of Migration from Kerala

As already stated certain pre-conditions should emerge for the actual beginnings of the process of migration. Even in Europe the era of migratory movement ushered in only with the break up of the old order. In India, the starting point was made with the changes in the attitude of the people towards material comforts. Migratory movement was delayed if not absent from Kerala because of the grip of certain powerful constraints. The constraints as stated earlier, were the existence of some sort of subsistence economic conditions, limited number of wants for the bulk of the people, extremely low level of population growth, rigid socio-economic structure etc. These constraints were actually the factors which also retarded the economic development. As a matter of fact, so long as the constraints were strong, there was neither development of the economy, nor migration of the people in search of better economic prospects. With the loosening of the constraints, the economy also began to display signs of development and expansion. Migration also started with the expansion of the economy. Then the question is, what were the forces which triggered the process of development of the economy?

Development is a socio-economic process in which, a change in one factor, as Myrdal puts, "is bound to bring a change in the other factor too and start a cumulative process of mutual interaction in which the change in one factor would continuously be supported by the reaction of the other factor and so in a circular way".[41] Such a circular causation leads not only to the development but also to a process of migratory movement.

In Kerala, as already mentioned, some sort of a subsistence economy prevailed in the past. One of the basic requirements for the development of a subsistence economy is a change in the attitude of the people towards material comforts. Once the attitude changes, people would be prepared to exert themselves more vigorously and even to move out of their rustic habitations in search of better economic prospects. In other words, a development consciousness in the place of subsistence mindedness is needed as a starting point.

Education, is one of the crucial factors which can create a change in the attitude in the minds of the people. With the spread of education, progressive ideas conducive to development would be inculcated in the minds of the people and gradually the barriers to development would crumble. Modern system of education had an earlier start in Kerala. It could however, make rapid progress only towards the close of nineteenth century.[42] The rapid growth of the mass media which began to appear from the closing decades of nineteenth century reinforced the influence of education in spreading new ideas, supporting new values and bringing people from different parts of the world into close contact.[43] The inevitable change in the attitude and behavioural pattern of the people resulting from these developments became visible during the years following the First World War. They were manifested in the desire of the people to have qualitative improvement in food, clothing and housing. Simultaneously, those who could afford for better amenities began to acquire them in proportion to their means. New ventures conducive to increase income earning prospects like joint stock companies, plantations, commercial farming, banking etc. were started. Thus a process of development was ushered in Kerala from the early decades of twentieth century.[44]

Migration also ensued as a concomitant to the process of development. One category of the migrants were the newly educated class who were not able to secure employment which corresponded to their educational qualifications and who were at the same time keen to improve their economic prospects. Not surprisingly, one Dewan of Travancore ridiculed the educated youth as worshippers of shirt for their reluctance to pursue the traditional occupations. Not only the educated class, but also the peasantry of Travancore set on a migratory movement in search of land suitable for extending cash crop cultivation. A close parallel is the migratory movement of Akwapim men of Ghana towards the close of nineteenth century. As in the case of Keralites, it was as Polly Hill puts, "the expansive set of wants set in motion through education, travel, and contact with others of conditions in other parts of the world" which instigated the Akwapim men to resort to a process of migration.[45]

The migratory movement thus started began to commence from different parts of Kerala since the turn of the century. Table 2.2 indicates the number of persons moved to different parts of India and foreign lands as on 1921.

As can be seen from the Table migrants from Travancore moved in different directions. Though not in large numbers, there were migrants in Europe, America, Australia, Mesopotomia, Persia, China and Africa. The list also includes, the number of migrants to Burma, Malaya and Ceylon, the traditional destination of migrants from India during the nineteenth century.

Significantly, the beginnings of migration to the Gulf region, which was destined to become an important destination in the years to come was made with the migration of Travancoreans to Mesopotamia. This migration took place under certain special circumstances. Mesopotamia which was part of the Turkish empire became a British Protectorate at the end of the First World War. A large number of skilled workers were required for the repair and maintenance of the infrastructural facilities of the country damaged by the war. Since local hands with sufficient experience and skill for the reconstruction of water and transport facilities were not available, skilled hands had to be recruited from countries like India. As many as 138,000 Indian labourers with sufficient skill were inducted soon after the War for this purpose.[46] A few Travancoreans who came to know of the openings, proceeded to that country. Significantly, as stated earlier, the migration to Mesopotamia could attract the attention of the Census Commissioner in 1921 who commented upon it as a turning point in the attitude towards the migratory movement of the Travancoreans.[47]

In sharp contrast to this, the Census Report 1901 contains an altogether different observation:

> "They cling to their families with persistence and so long as they can eke out an existence in the vicinity of their own houses, the desire to venture abroad rarely occurs to them".[48]

Needless to say, a perceptible change has taken place in the attitude of Travancoreans towards migration within a short period of twenty years.

Table 2.2: Volume of Migration from Different Parts of Kerala in 1921

Sl. No.	*Place of Destination*	*Migrants from Travancore*	*Migrants from Cochin*	*Migrants from Malabar District*
1.	Madras city	—	867	5995
2.	Madras presidency	2479	9257	32080
3.	Mysore	178	367	—
4.	Bombay	220	479	—
5.	Bengal	77	222	—
6.	Delhi	3	3	—
7.	Others parts of India	157	187	—
8.	Burma	251	155	—
9.	Ceylon	2783	4056 *	—
10.	Singapore	1467	-	—
11.	Federated Malaya	275	25	—
12.	Mesopotomia	395	-	—
13.	Other parts of Asia	202	33	—
14.	United Kingdom	28	27	—
15.	Other parts of Europe	7	18	—
16.	Africa	19	—	—
17.	Australia	3	4	—
18.	America	6	3	—
19	Travancore/unknown	112	12366	
	Total	9342	24013 **	38075

Sources: 1. *Census of India, 1921*, Vol.XXX, Travancore
2. *Census of India, 1921*, Vol.I, Cochin
3. *Census of India, 1921*, Vol.XII, Madras, Part I.

Notes: * Relates to 1911
** Total does not include the migrants to Ceylon.

Significantly, migration also started to the other parts of the world like Europe, Great Britain, America, Australia etc. One of the prominent migrants to Europe was Chempakaraman Pillai, a renowned freedom fighter who opted to fight with the Germans against the British during the First World war for the purpose of liberating India from the clutches of British imperialism.[49] Another noted Malayalee migrant was Sri K.P. Kesava Menon who reached Great Britain for the purpose of education in 1912.[50]

Migratory movement of similar nature also commenced from the Cochin state. Emigration figures of those who went to foreign lands are scanty. However, according to the 1911 Census, there were not less than 5000 persons of Cochin origin working in Ceylon. Interestingly, Malayalees in Ceylon were labelled as *Cochiyans*.[51] As can be seen from the Table emigrants from these two states included those who moved to Mumbai, Chennai and the former Mysore state. However, there were very few persons from these two states in any of those places in 1901. Significantly, Travancoreans and Cochinites also began to migrate to Delhi which became the Imperial Capital in 1911. There were 3 persons of Cochin origin and 3 persons of Travancore origin in Delhi.

No separate figures relating to the migration to other parts of India from the Malabar distrct are available. However, the number of Malabar born persons enumerated in other parts of the Madras presidency was pretty high. It stood at 38,075 in 1921. On the other hand, the number of persons born in Malabar district but enumerated in other parts of the Presidency was 17,756 in 1901. In Madras city proper, the number which was only 1666 in 1901 increased to 5995 by 1921.[52]

Linguistic distribution of population in areas outside Kerala forms another source of data on migration. Malayalam speaking population in other parts of India except a few living in the border areas of Kerala can be either the migrants or their descendants from Kerala. The total population in other parts of the Madras presidency except in South Canara and Nilgiris was only 7246 persons in 1901.[53] The number increased to 19,264 by 1921.[54] There was thus an increase of more than 265 per cent. Such an increase might be due to the spurt in the volume of migration between 1901 and 1921. In Madras city proper the increase was from 804 in 1901 to 4043 in 1921. The volume of migration on the basis of birth place returns was much more than under linguistic distribution. This must be due to the presence of a large number of non-Malayalam speaking population like the Pattar Brahmins among the migrants from Kerala who speak Tamil as their mother tongue.

The number of Malayalam speaking population in Mysore state also recorded appreciable increase. The increase was from 3811 in 1901 to 5811 in 1921. Most of the Malayalees concentrated in centres like Kadur, Hassan and Kolar. While Kadur and Hassan were centres of coffee cultivation, Kolar was a gold mining centre. Most of the Malayalees were labourers employed in the plantation at Kadur- Hassan region and in the gold mines at Kolar. A good number of the migrants were petty traders and hawkers. Most of them were Mappilla Muslims who migrated because of the frequent outbreaks of Mappilla riots in Malabar during the nineteenth century and the consequent oppressive policies pursued by the British rulers to suppress such agitation. As a result, the Mappillas, as Innes puts, "emigrated to Mysore goldfields, worked in the railways which were being constructed and even went as far a field as Ceylon, the Strait Settlement and the Dutch Indies for trade".[55]

Compared to Travancore or Cochin, the intensity of migration was very high in Malabar. Majority of the Malayalees in distant lands were from Malabar. In Bombay for example, out of the 1210 persons born in Kerala, but enumerated in Bombay, as many as 1063 were from Malabar in 1901.[56] The persons born in Travancore were only 57 and of Cochin 90. A number of factors accounted for such high intensity of migration from Malabar. First, Malabar formed part of the then Madras presidency. Persons born in Malabar had naturally to move to Madras for various administrative purposes. Second, the opening of Malabar to other parts of India made it easy for people from Malabar to migrate to other parts of India. The third condition was the unequitable distribution of land rights. In the opinion of Gangulee, "the great volume of migration takes place from the regions where the disharmony of the agrarian economy has become acute, and that the underlying causes of emigration are survial of the antiquated system of land tenure".[57] The land tenure system which prevailed in Malabar during the British colonial period was not at all equitable by any standard. Practically, the entire area of land including wastelands and forest lands was under the ownership of non-cultivating landlords. The actual cultivation was being carried on by rent paying tenants who became a pauperized class on account of the exhorbitant rate of rent and other dues by the landowners. The tenants could be evicted by the landlords on flimsy grounds and any extension of cultivation could be undertaken with the consent of the landlords under unfavourable conditions. On the other hand, the ownership of land was vested with the cultivating peasants under payment of land-tax directly to the government in Travancore. The system was very liberal and the land-tax was moderate. While the peasants and cultivating classes of Travancore could enrich themselves in course of time, the tenant farmers of Malabar were pauperised and marginalised. Any opportunity for migration to distant lands was naturally a safety valve to the pauperized tenant and to the impoverised classes in Malabar. The intensity of migration was naturally very high from Malabar than from Travancore or Cochin. Not surprisingly, more number of migrants from Malabar can be found in places away from Kerala like Madras or Mumbai or Mysore or in foreign lands than from Travancore or Cochin.

Notwithstanding the beginnings of migratory movements from the early decades of twentieth century, Travancore and Cochin states were receiving more number of inmigrants rather than sending outmigrants. The net volume of inmigration to these two states was 9786 during the decade 1901-1911 and 20082 for the decade 1911-1921 respectively. In both the states inmigrants came to the newly opened plantations from the erstwhile Madras presidency. Zachariah who has examined this issue makes the following obervation: "In many social and demographic respects Travancore-Cochin had the characteristics of an outmigrating area, but its location near a state with high outmigration plus the hospitality offered to the migrants by its rulers made it as an area of inmigration. Tea and rubber estates in Travancore were a source of employment to many Tamilians from Madras who were specially skilled in plantation works".[58] If so, the question is, why were demographic pressure and opening of plantation not sufficiently strong to countervail the inmigration flow? The answer to the question will be examined in the context internal migration in Kerala.

In sum, the beginnings of migration were made when a wide range of changes conducive to migratory movement took place. However, there was wide variations in the intensity of migration from region to region. The volume of migration was much bigger from Malabar than from Travancore or Cochin. Further, Travancore and Cochin on the other hand remained as inmigratory regions in spite of the emergence of an era of migratory movement.

Notes and References

1. Valavanthara, Antony; *India in 1500 AD: Translation of the Narratives of Joseph the Indian* (Mannanam, Rishi Institute, 1984), p. 184.
2. Ravenstein, E.G., "Laws of Migration" in *Journal of Royal Statistical Society, 1885.*
3. Lee, Everett, S., "A Theory of Migration" in *Demography* Vol.3, No.3, 1966.
4. See: (a) Lewis, Arthur W.A.; "Economic Development with Unlimited Supplies of Labour" in *Manchesor School of Economics and Social Studies*, May 1954.
   (b) Fei, JCH & Ranis, G., "A Theory of Economic Development" in the *American Economic Review*, Vol.5, 1961.
   (c) Todaro, M.P., "A Model of Labour Migration and Urban Unemployment in Less Developed Countries", in *American Economic Review*, March 1969.
5. Sjaastad, Larry S., "The Cost and Returns of Human Migration" in *Journal of Political Economy*, Oct. 1962, Part II.
6. T.G. Mc Gee, "Rural Labour Mobility in South and South East Asia" in William H. Mcneill and Adam Ruth (S), *Human Migration Patterns and Policies* (Indiana University Press 1978), pp.202-4.
7. Wood, Charles S., "Equilibrium and Historical Structural Perspective in Migration" in *International Migration Review*, Vol.XVI, No. 2, 1982.
8. Zelinsky, Wilbur., "The Hypothesis on Mobility Transition" in *Geographical Review* (61, 1971).

9. Prejor, Robin J., "Integrating Internal and External Migration Theories" in Kritz, Mary M. *Global Trends in Migration* (New York, Centre for Migration Studies, 1986), p. 124.
10. See Chapter 1, p. 5.
11. M.S.A. Rao., "Some Aspects of Sociology of Migration" in M.S.A Rao (ed). *Studies in Migration* (Delhi, Manohar, 1986), p. 31.
12. Mukerjee, Radhakamal, *The Foundations of Indian Economics* (London, Longman Green & Co., 1910), p. 3.
13. Ward and Conner, *Geographical and Statistical Memoirs of the Survey of Travancore and Cochin States* (Trivandrum, Government Press, 1863), p. 90.
14. Aiya, Nagam V., *Travancore State Manual Vol.III* (Trivandrum, Government Press, 1905), p. 114.
15. Shea, Thomas W., "Economic Development in Traditional Societies - Malabar: A Case Study" in *Journal of Economic History*, Vol. 19, 1959.
16. *Report of the Census of Travancore, 1891* (Trivandrum, Government Press, 1893), p. 234.
17. Davis, Kingsley, *Population of India and Pakistan* (New Jersey, Princeton University Press, 1951), pp. 102-104.
18. C. Kondapi: *Indians in Overseas 1838-1949* (Oxford University Press, 1951), p. 4.
19. W. Crooke, *Natives of Northern India* (London, 1907), pp. 10-11.
20. Quoted by K.S. Gillon in Fiji's: *Indian Migration* (Melbourne, Oxford University Press 1962), p. 46 from W. Crooke, *Natives of Northern India* (London, 1907).
21. C. Kondapi, *op.cit.*, p. 5.
22. *Report of the Indian Labour Emigration to Ceylon and Malaya* (Madras Government Press, 1917), p. 7 and p. 30.
23. Panchanan Saha: *Repatriation of Indian Lbour 1834-1900* (New Delhi, People's Publishing House, 1970), p. 46.
24. *Census of Madras Presidency, 1901, Vol.I*, p. 32.
25. *G.O.No. 377, Public dated 17 May 1907* (Archives Madras).
26. *Proceedings No.34 Pub dated 34d July 1903 of the Govt. of Madras* (Archives, Delhi).
27. *Census of India 1901, Vol.XII, A Burma: Imperial Tables.*
28. J.C. Jha, *Aspects of Indentured Inland Emigration to North-East India 1859-1908* (New Delhi: Indus Publishing Company, 1996), p. 28.
29. J.C. Jha, *op.cit.*, p. 145
30. Davis Kingsley, *op.cit.*, p. 103.
31. Kondapi, C.
32. *Appendix to Statistical Atlas to Madras Presidency 1901.*
33. Handlin, Oscar, *the Uprooted: The Epic Story of Great Migration that Made the American People* (Asian Book, New Delhi 1973), p. 22.
34. Mukerjee, Radhakamal, *op.cit.*, p. 5.
35. Davis, Kingsley, *op.cit.* p. 103.

36. Quoted by Findlay Shirras, in "Indian Migration" in Walter F. Willcox: *International Migration, Vol.II Interpretation* (New York, Gorden Reach Publishers, 1969), p. 598.
37. Davis Kingsley, *op.cit.*, p. 103.
38. Daniel, Roger: "The Indian Diaspora in the United States" in Judith Brown (ed.) *Migration, the Indian Experience* (Oxford, St Martin's, Press, 1994), p. 85.
39. John Hinnels: "The Modern Zorastrian Diaspora" in Judith Brown, et.al. *op.cit.* p. 61.
40. Myrdal, Gunnar: *Asian Drama* (Pelican Book 1972), p. 972.
41. Myrdal, Gunnar, *Economic Theory of Underdevelopment* (London, Gerald Duckworth & Co., Ltd. 1957), p. 13.
42. The number of students enrolled in the schools of Travancore which was only 0.6 lakhs in 1893-94, increased to 1.5 lakhs by 1903-04 and to about 5 lakhs by 1925. See *Administration Report of Travancore* for Various Years. Similar increase took place in Malabar and Cochin also.
43. Malayalam Newpapers, (1) Deepika was started in 1884, (2) Malayala Manorama 1893, (3) Kerala Kaumudi in 1913 and (4) Mathrubhoomi in 1922.
44. K.V. Joseph, *Culture and Industrial Development: Indian Experience* (New Delhi, Anmol Publications, 2004), pp. 44-45.
45. Hill, Polly., *Migrant Cocoa Farmers of Southern Ghana* (Cambridge University Press, 1976), p. 168.
46. Letter dated Feb. 19, 1919 from Viceroy of India to Montage, Secretary of State for India (Archives, Delhi).
47. *Census of India 1921, Travancore Part I* (Trivandrum, Government Press), p. 28.
48. *Census of India 1901, Travancore Part I* (Trivandrum, Government Press), p. 227.
49. Jensen Joan M. *Passage from India: Asian Indian Immigrants in North America* (New Haven, Yale University Press, 1988), p. 200.
50. K.P. Kesava Menon, the founder editor of *Mathrubhoomi*, a leading newspaper in Malayalam was in Great Britain from July 1912 to August 1915. Details of his visit and experiences in Great Britain and other European countries were published in *Bilathi Vishesham* (Mal) (*Information on Europe)* (Kozhikode, Mathrubhoomi Printing and Publishing Co. Ltd. Reprint 1983).
51. A.K. Gopalan, *In the Cause of the People Reminiscences* (Delhi, Orient Longman 1973), p. 126.
52. *Census of Madras 1921, Part II Imperial Tables, Birth Place.*
53. Kasargod taluk of the South old Canara district was a predominantly Malayalam speaking region. Gudalur taluk in Nilgiris was owned by a feudal house of Malabar. Naturally, there were large number of Malayalam speaking population in Gudalur taluk.
54. *Census of Madras Presidency Part II Imperial Tables.*

55. C.A. Innes, *Madras District Gazetteers, Malabar and Anjengo* (Madras, Superintendent, Government Press, 1908) p. 86.
56. *Census of India Vol.XI, Bombay Town and Island Part VI Tables, Table XI Birth Place* (Bombay Times of India Press, 1901).
57. Gangulee, N. *Indians in the Empire Overseas: A Survey* (London, New India Publishing House, 1947), p. 228.
58. K.C. Zachariah: *A Historical Study of Internal Migration in the Indian Sub-continent 1901-1931* (Bombay, Asia Publishing House, 1964), p. 209.

Chapter 3

Migration to Foreign Lands

In the previous chapter we have examined the constraints which retarded migratory movement in India and how certain patterns of migration could emerge inspite of the constraints. How the constraints were eroded in course of time and the manner in which different patterns of migration could originate with the erosion of the constraints were also examined in the case of India as a whole and Kerala in particular. The theme of this Chapter is to examine the trends in the external migration since then.

The dominant pattern of migration which took place during the nineteenth century was assisted labour migration under indenture system. Eventhough, indenture was the dominant pattern, certain other patterns, though on a limited scale also emerged. Indenture was full of abuses and there was strong resentment against the system. As a result, labour migration under indenture was banned by 1916.[1] However, migration including that of assisted labour under other systems was in full swing. A considerable number of Indians had migrated in various parts of the world by the early decades of twentieth century. The important countries of destination were Mauritius, South Africa, East African countries, British Guiana, Caribbean Islands, Fiji, Malaya, Ceylon and Burma. Table 3.1 given below indicates the total number of Indian population in those countries as on 1921.

As the Table indicates, the largest number of Indians was in Burma, which was administered as part of India till 1935. The second largest contingent was in Ceylon, followed by Malaya. In these three countries, migration was under *Kangani* or *Sardari* or *Maistry* systems, which were for practical purposes different variants of the indenture system. Migration to Mauritius, West Indies, South Africa, Fiji, Guiana etc. where a sizeable number of Indians were found, was under indenture system. With the abolition of indenture system migration to these countries came to an end. The abolition of indenture system was not the only reason for the discontinuance of migration to these countries. Demand for migrant labour reached a saturation point in all these

Table 3.1: Indian Population in Various Foreign Lands as on 1921

Sl.No.	*Name of the Country*	*Numbers in Thousands*[1]
1.	Burma*[2]	887.0
2.	Ceylon	640.0
3.	Malaya	472.0
4.	Mauritius	266.0
5.	South Africa	161.0
6.	East African Countries	65.0
7.	West Indies, Jamaica etc.	147.0
8.	British Guiana	125.0
9.	Fiji	61.0
10.	Great Britain	82.0
11.	U.S.A.	5.0
12.	Canada	1.2
13.	Australia	2.0
14.	Egypt	1.0
15.	Others	3.02
	Total	2918.22

Sources: 1. Findlay Shirras, "Indian Migration" in Water Willcox *International Migration*, Vol.II, p.592.[2]

2. N.R.Chakravarti, *The Indian Minority in Burma* (Oxford University Press,m 1971), p.15.[3]

* Burma was included as part of India till 1935.

countries by 1920s. On the other hand, streams of migrants continued to pour into Malaya, Burma and Ceylon inspite of the termination of indenture system.

Indian migrants were also found in U.K., the U.S.A., Canada and Australia; though not in large numbers. Most of them were from Punjab, Gujarat, Bengal and other north Indian regions. Keralites were very few in all these countries.

Gulf region was yet to emerge as an important destination of Indian migrants in 1920, though as stated in the previous chapter, thousands of Indians were inducted in the civil and military establishments in Mesopotomia immediately after the First World War. However, it was destined to become an important destination of migrants in the years to come. Though, migration to Malaya and Sri Lanka was essentially a Tamil phenomenon and to Burma a Bengali or Telugu phenomenon, considerable number of Malayalees were also found in these countries. As already seen in Chapter 2, Malayalees began to flock to these countries from the dawn of twentieth century. A brief account of Indian migration to these countries, to the countries of the Gulf region and to the U.S. would be attempted in the following sections.

BURMA (Myanmar)

Burma (Myanmar) is one of the countries in which fairly large scale migration took place from India since the middle of nineteenth century. Burma was part of the British colonial empire and was administered as a province of India till 1935. Contact between India and Burma dates back to the pre-historic period. Migration was taking place on a small scale from India for centuries and the migrants from India were absorbed as part of the Burmese society. Naturally, no separate identity could be maintained by the Indians in Burma in the past.

With the British conquest of Burma during nineteenth century, migratory movement of the modern period started from India. During the initial stages, Indians were camp followers of the British who used their services in setting up the administration, in enforcing law and order, and in all kinds of inferior services. Soon after the conquest of lower Burma, the British authorities embarked on a massive development programme of Iravady delta, till then a marshy land sparsely populated. What they did was to convert the water-logged marshy lands into paddy fields. The scheme was to assign the lands to various categories of people including Indians who could induct capital for the purpose of reclamation. Simultaneously, attempts were made to develop Rangoon, then a sleepy village of hardly 9000 inhabitants into a major port and commercial centre. Labour force of different categories was required for both purposes. Since, enough labour force of Burmese origin was not forthcoming for these gigantic programmes, the authorities turned to India as a source for the supply of labour. Thus started the migration of the Indians workers on a fairly large scale.[4] Migration of the Indians was encouraged by providing certain incentives and concessions.

Side by side, demand for technical hands also arose for the purpose of handling the newly opened transport, water supply, railway, electricity distribution schemes, etc. Since Burmese workers with technical know-how and experience were not available in sufficient numbers, services of Indians were sought. The migration thus started, gained momentum within a short period. The volume of Indian population in Burma over the years was as given in Table 3.2.

As can be seen from the Table, the migrants constituted about 7 percent of the population. According to Chakravarti, the census data do not convey the real size of migrant population, as a large number of seasonal workers arriving in Burma during harvest season were also included in the census figures. According to him, the Indian population did not exceed 5 per cent of the Burmese population at any period.[5]

Table 3.2: Growth of Indian Population in Burma over the Years

Year	*Indian Population*	*Indian population as a percentage to the total population of Burma*
1881	243,123	6.5
1891	420,830	5.1
1901	568,263	5.4
1911	743,288	6.1
1921	887,077	6.7
1931	1,017,825	6.9
1941	918,000	5.4

Source: Adapted from N.R.Chakravarti, *The Indian Minority in Burma* (Oxford University Press: Institute of Race Relations, 1971), p. 15.

However, in Rangoon, which has grown as a major commercial city by the end of nineteenth century, Indian population totalled 130000, which formed roughly half the population of that city in 1901.[6]

Burmese sentiment was hostile towards Indians from the very beginning and they regarded Indians as part of the repressive force of British administration. Since 1920s it began to surface in the open, and in turn led to racial riots of the worst types in 1930, 1931 and 1938, in which many Indians were killed and their properties looted. Burmese approach gave the impression that they were keen to separate from India than to gain political freedom. The Japanese attack and the occupation of Burma took place when the anti-Indian feeling was at its high pitch. Indians were the worst sufferers during the Japanese occupation and nearly 500,000 Indians left on foot to India; many of them dying during the journey.[7] At the end of the war, Burma did not tolerate any further Indian migration and many Indians especially in "the services" were compelled to leave Burma after opting out for voluntary retirement at not very favourable terms. In independent Burma, Indians were not accorded with any minority status and only a tiny minority among them could secure citizenship with great difficulty. Those who opted to remain in Burma with small shops and business enterprises were hit hard when Burma nationalised all business activities under the Burmese socialism of Gen Newin.

Classes of Indians in Burma

Broadly speaking, the Indian migrants consisted of three classes of people. The first category consisted of the capitalist communities which included mostly the Chettiars, Parsis and Marwaris. Though they did not form a numerically large section, they contributed much to the economic development of Burma and in turn wielded considerable influence in the economy. The second category consisted of teachers, professionals, doctors, engineers, lawyers, accountants, clerical and supervisory staff etc. The vast majority of the Indians belonged to the labouring class both skilled and unskilled. There was great demand for such labour classes as enough Burmans were not ready to take up such works.[8] Most of the workers in the railways, transport, water supply and such other skilled services were also of Indian origin as Burmese were not sufficiently experienced with skill to take up such activities.

Linguistic Composition of the Indians in Burma

Migrants to Burma hailed from different parts of India. The composition of Indian population in Burma on linguistic basis was as given in Table 3.3.

As can be seen from the Table, Bengalis topped the list followed by Hindi speaking population, Tamils, Telugus, Oriyas, Punjabis and Gujaratis in the discending order. The Bengalis were mostly from Chittagong and they were called as Chittagongians. Hindi speaking population hailed mainly from Sultanpur and Fyzabad. Tamils were from Ramnad and Tanjore and Telugus were chiefly from Ganjam, Godavari and Vizag. The Tamils included a large number of Chettiars who invested their capital on a fairly large scale in various commercial ventures.

As can be seen, Malayalees formed only an insigificant proportion accounting for 1.17 per cent of the total migrants from India in 1931.

Table 3.3: Linguistic Composition of Indian Population in Burma in 1931

Linguistic Group	*Males*	*Females*	*Total*
Tamil	118659	65448	184107 (17.76)
Telugu	124483	36157	160640 (15.49)
Oriya	57247	3435	60682 (5.85)
Bengali	242415	134579	376994 (36.37)
Hindi	145589	46978	192567 (18.57)
Punjabi	20639	7270	27909 (2.69)
Gujarati	12511	5195	17706 (1.70)
Malayalee	11343	875	12218 (1.17)
Others	2648	1070	3718 (0.35)
Total	735534	301007	1036541 (100)

Source: *Census of India 1931, Vol.II*, Imperial Tales, Table XV, *Languages*.[9]

Note: 1. Others include Canarese, Sindhis, Marathis, Konkanis, Biharis, Assamese, and Rajasthanis.

2. Figures in the bracket indicate percentage.

However, the ranks of Malayalee migrants were increasing at a fast rate since the turn of the century. As seen earlier, their number formed only 324 in 1901. It increased to 5926 by 1921 and to 12218 in 1931.[10] The increase was more than 40 times within a short period of thirty years in 1931. However, migration from Kerala gathered momentum at a time when anti-Indian feeling was very high among the Burmese. As a consequence, most of the Keralites returned for good with the Japanese occupation of Burma by which time conditions became totally unsatisfactory. Very few among them went back to Burma at the end of the War, as the attitude of the Burmese government became by and large unfriendly towards the Indian migrants. Among the different linguistic groups from India the Malayalee component had the least female sex ratio in Burma. There were only 832 females in 1931 against 11343 males which accounted for a very low female ratio of 8 per cent. Apparently, the bulk of the Malayalee immigrants were mere sojourners who reached Burma for enriching themselves. Significantly, as reported by Adrian Mayer it was the migrants who returned from Burma were those who started to construct posh-type buildings in Malabar.[11]

The bulk of the migrants were from Malabar region as the number of migrants from Travancore was only 251 and from Cochin 155 in 1921.[12] Even in 1931, there were only 816 migrants from Travancore and 239 from Cochin.[13] The rest constituting more than 90 per cent would have been from Malabar. Further, most of the migrants numbering more than 9000, were Moplah Muslims of Malabar. A good many among them were petty hawkers, shop-keepers and street vendors. Migrants from Kerala also occupied technical, clerical, administrative and supervisory categories of occupations.

MALAYSIA

Contact between India and Malaya was very strong for centuries in the past. Traders and priests used to frequent Malayan peninsula and Malayan culture itself was moulded by Indian culture. However, much of the cultural contact decayed since the Muslim conquest of India. It was restored with the establishment of British hegemony in India. Migration from India also revived since then.

When the British officers arrived in Penang one of the offshore islands of Malaya in 1786, they were accompanied by Indian domestic servants and camp-followers apart from lascars and sepoys. Other labourers were not far behind to follow. According to an authority there were one thousand Indian shop keepers and coolies settled in the island by early 1790, in addition to the annual arrival of 1300-2000 men in Malaya through the vessels sailing from Coromandel coast..[14]

Different Categories of Migrants

Demand for labour arose on an increasing scale with the beginning of spice cultivation in 1790, followed by sugar in 1830, coffee in 1870 and rubber in the early years of the 20th century. The introduction of oil palm and tea at a subsequent date accelerated the demand further. Infrastructural development of roads and railways also called for the service of large number of workers with sufficient technical skill.

Of the different kinds of people, the south Indian peasants particularly of the low caste Madrasees were considered the most suitable class for service in Malaya as they were malleable, less ambitious, and could work well under supervision and could be easily managed. The agreeable climate of Malaya with that of south India also was a favourable factor. The Europeans who initiated various innovative enterprises had enough experience with the south Indian labour in the plantations and road and railway construction workshops of Ceylon. Indian labourers were sought also to check the growing Chinese influence. These favourable conditions facilitated the smooth flow of labour migrants from south India.[15] For a long period, the workers were recruited under *Kangani* system for which active support and encouragement was extended by the *Sirkar*. Since the *Kangani* system and other forms of assisted labour migration were full of abuses they were dispensed with by 1920s and migrants moved subsequently under free labour migration.

Most of the labour migrants hailed from Chinglupet, North Arcot, Trichinopoly, Tanjore, Salem and South Arcot districts of former Madras presidency. Migration also took place from Malabar district. However, migrants from Malabar district formed hardly 6 per cent of the total migrants from the Madras presidency during the period 1923-1930.[16]

With the establishment of British colonial administration in Malaya, day-to-day business of the government and various commercial departments and agencies came to be conducted mainly in English. But English education was slow to spread in Malaya. Not only general, but also technical education was late to be started. As a result, the government agencies and private employees had no choice but to recruit English speaking junior staff from places outside Malaya. The choice fell on south India and Ceylon where English education had an earlier start. At the same time, enough employment opportunities were not available in these regions to absorb the growing ranks of the educated youth. Naturally, many among the educated classes opted to move to Malaya in order to seek employment as office assistants, teachers, technicians, supervisors and skilled workers in various government departments, railway projects, naval establishments, private enterprises and so on. Some of them were able to get absorbed in clerical, supervisory and managerial cadres in the plantations and private enterprises also.[17]

As the south Indians were sought after for clerical and such other categories of occupations, the north Indians particularly the Sikhs were inducted to take up employment in those occupations likc that of soldiers, policemen, taxi drivers, etc. The Sikhs on their part had proved their calibre in these occupations in other parts of the empire like Hongkong. With the spread of fame of the first batch of Sikh soldiers who reached Malaya in 1881, they were sought after by various private agencies.[18]

In addition, petty entrepreneurs, moneylenders, merchants, traders and such other people also arrived in Malaya. Traders and hawkers were endowed with capital and experience. Gradually, professionals like doctors, lawyers, teachers etc. also arrived in small batches.

Trends in the Flow of Migration

The different patterns of migration thus started, gained momentum since the turn of the century. While there was strong anti-Indian feeling in the neighbouring Myanmar, Indians were welcomed wholeheartedly in Malaya and were bestowed with dignified status in the Malayan society. Table 3.4 given below indicates the growth of Indian population in Malaya over the years.

Table 3.4: Growth of Indian Population in Malaya and Singapore Over the Years

Year	*No. of Indians in various parts of Malaya*	*No. of Indians in Singapore*	*Total*	*Percentage increase*
1881	31,862	12,138	44,000	—
1891	59,965	16,035	76,000	56.5
1901	101,155	17,845	119,000	56.5
1911	239,815	28,454	268,269	125.4
1921	437,493	32,687	470,180	75.2
1931	578,987	50,860	621,847	32.2
1947	530,638	68,978	599,616	-3.6
1957	696,186	124,084	820,270	36.7

Source: *Adapted from Kernail Singh Sandhu,* Indians in Malaya (*Cambridge University Press, 1969*), p. 183.

As the Table indicates, there was steady increase in the volume of Indian population in Malaya except for the period 1931-1947. The fall in the size of Indian population in the thirties was due to the Japanese occupation of Malaya. There was an increase in the size of Indian population since 1947 in contrast to the fall in Ceylon or Burma. Indians formed approximately 5 to 6 per cent of the Malayan population during nineteenth century. Since the turn of 20th century, they constituted approximately 10 per cent of the population in Malaya.

Linguistic Composition of the Indian Population in Malaya

As already stated, migrants from India belonged to different ethnic-cum-linguistic groups. Table 3.5 indicates the linguistic composition of Indian population during the twentieth century.

Table 3.5: Linguistic Composition of the Indian Population in Malaya and Singapore

Sl. No.	*Linguistic Groups*	*Number of persons belonging to different linguistic groups of Indian origin in Malaysia*				
		1921	*1931*	*1947*	*1957*	*1970***
1.	Tamils	387,500	514,778	460,985	634,681	746,558
2.	Malayalees	17,190	34,898	44,339	72,971	44,199
3.	Telugus	39,986	32,536	24,093	27,670	31,332
4.	Punjabis	15,451	—	30,952	N.A.	72,138
5.	Others	10,043	—	—	20,000	
	Total	470,180	621,847*	599,616*	820,270*	894,227*

Source: *Adapted from Kernial Singh Sandhu, op.cit.*, p. 237.

* There is some discrepancy in the totals as the data relating to "others" are incomplete.

** From S. Rajoo, Indians in Peninsular Malaysia in I.J. Bahadur Singh (ed.) *Indians in South East Asia* (New Delhi, Sterling Publishers Pvt. Ltd., 1982) p. 54.

As can be seen from the Table, the size of the ethnic Indian population has been increasing steadily since 1921 except for a marginal fall in1947 which was apparently due to the difficulties created by the Second World War. Among the Indians, the Tamils formed the largest group accounting for about 80 per cent of the total Indian population.

The size of Malayalee immigrants which accounting for hardly 4 per cent of the ethnic Indians in Malaysia in 1921 totalled 17,100, has been growing at a fast rate. By 1957 they formed nearly 10 per cent of the Indian population in Malaya. However, there was a sharp fall since then and by 1970 they formed hardly 5 per cent of the Indians in Malaya. The actual number of Malayalees totalled only 44,199 in 1970 against 72,971 in 1957.

There would have been many reasons for the fall in the size of the Malayalee population in Malaya by 1970. First, some of the Malayalees would have left Malaya on account of the restrictions imposed for acquiring citizenship to the immigrants with the attainment of independence of Malaya. Malayalees as a class were reluctant to take up citizenship as to be inferred from the following observation of a well informed authority.

"Of the Indians in Malaya, the Malayalees appear to have been the least anxious to bring their womenfolk with them. Their sex-ratio was the lowest in 1957, with about 480 females only for every 1000 males compared with more than 900:1000 female-male ratio of Telugus. They are the least settled Indian group in Malaya and many of them even to this day generally seem to regard Malaya as a place to earn an income to support families in India".[19]

Another reason would have been the separation of Singapore from Malaya. Proportionately more Malayalees were to be found in Singapore. There were as many as 24,000 Malayalees in Singapore in 1970.[20] If we add this figure with the number of Malayalee population in Malaya, there would not be an appreciable fall in the percentage of Malayali population in 1970.

While the overwhelming majority of the Tamils were estate workers, Malayalees as a class were employed as civilian clerks, junior officers in government offices and British War dispartinents, and as clerks, conductors and assistants in the European owned rubber, oil palm and other plantations. Since English education had an earlier start in Kerala, the educated persons who could secure those jobs in Malaya opted to migrate from the early decades of twentieth century. They could easily supplant the Tamils from Madras and Jaffna and occupy junior supervisory positions in various establishments. Once settled in Malaya, they were keen to set up their own networks and induct their own friends and relatives. The following excerpts from the findings of a study clearly illustrate how one of the earliest migrants from Kerala reached Malaya and how he subsequently brought his relatives and friends to Malaya.

"One K.C. George from Ayiroor, 10-12 kilometers from Koipuram is generally identified to be the first person to emigrate to Malaya in recent decades. In Kozhikode, where he was learning typewriting and short-hand after passing his matriculation examination from a high school in his own locality, he came to know of the employment opportunities in British plantations in Malaya which were started in 1900—. However, many people from Kozhikode region also came to know about the availability of jobs and started emigrating to Malaya.

This is what gave Mr.George the idea and inspiration to migrate. He came back home from Kozhikode and left for Malaya in 1911 from the Madras port. On each of his subsequent visits home from Malaya he took with him about a dozen people or so to work in different plantation companies there".[21]

The ranks of Malayalees also included estate workers. However, the proportion was very low. While Tamils, formed the overwhelming majority of estate workers, Malayalee element formed hardly 5 per cent.[22] In fact, majority of the Tamils migrated to Malaya when assisted labour migration was prevalent. On the other hand, migration from Kerala became brisk only after the abolition of indentured labour and other forms of assisted labour migration. Since Keralites were better placed they did not suffer much during Japanese occupation. They could rise in social ladder as they were better educated. It is not surprising that Mr.Devan Nair, an emigrant from Kerala could become the President of Singapore. It may be mentioned in this connection that most of the workers involved in the construction of Singapore Naval base were from Kerala.[23] They formed roughly 80 per cent of the construction workers. Devan Nair was one of the trade union leaders of Singapore before he became a political leader. The ranks of Malayalees also included salesmen, streetside vendors, stall holders, hawkers etc. It was the Mappilla Muslims from Malabar who formed the bulk of such category of migrants from Kerala.

Among the three regions of Kerala, the largest contingent of migrants was from Malabar. According to the Special Emigration data collected with the census of 1931, there were 2485 Cochin born persons in Malaya.[24] The number of persons emigrated from Travancore was around 4338 according to a special emigration survey conducted with the census of 1931.[25] The two would add upto a total number of 6823. As stated earlier, the total Malayalee population in Malaya was 34,898 in 1931. If we deduct 6823 being the total from Travancore and Cochin, from the total Malayalee population of 34,898, the balance would be from Malabar. Naturally, the number of persons from Malabar would be 28,075, being the balance after deducting the number of persons from Cochin and Travancore.

CEYLON (SRI LANKA)

Ceylon or Sri Lanka is one of the countries with which India had maintained close links from ancient past. Practically, all the inhabitants of Ceylon are of Indian origin who migrated either from northern part of India or southern part of India during ancient past. Migration during the modern period started with the introduction of coffee cultivation in Ceylon. It was estimated that as many as 10,000 Indian labourers were found working in the coffee plantations of Ceylon in 1837. The number went on swelling and by 1855 the number was stated to be 128,000.[26] Migratory movement continued to accelerate with the introduction of tea plantations during the succeeding years.

By and large, migration to Ceylon was a Tamil phenomenon. In the words of the Census Commissioner of 1931, "Ceylon is no more foreign to Trichinopoly labourer than Madras or Ramnad and very much less so than Malabar or Mysore".[27] The bulk of the migrants hailed from Trichinopoly, Tinnevely, Ramnad, Salem, Madurai and Pudukottai. Majority of them were estate workers. The volume of Indian population in Ceylon totalled 732,258 in 1946.[28]

Anti-Indian feeling was very strong in Ceylon since the turn of the century. Most of the Indian labourers were kept as stateless persons and citizenship right was granted only to a tiny minority. Majority of the Indian labourers were repatriated to India as a result of the Shastri-Sirimao Agreement of 1964.

Though migration to Ceylon was a Tamil phenomenon, a few Malayalees also managed to migrate to Sri Lanka from the early decades of the twentieth century. No accurate data are available on the magnitude of migration from Kerala. According to the Special Migration Table prepared with the Census of 1921, there were as many as 4259 Travancore born persons in Ceylon.[29] The Census Report of Cochin for the year 1911 mentions about the presence of 4056 Cochin born persons in Ceylon. The number of Cochin born persons appeared to have gone upto 9618 by 1931.[30] No wonder, Malayalees were generally referred to as 'Cochiyans' in Ceylon.[31] No separate figures are available about the volume of the migrant population from Malabar district. Most of them were from Ponnani taluk of the Malabar district. Unlike the Tamils who were mostly estate workers, the bulk of Malayalees were non-estate workers. There was also a small section of officers and middle class clerks among the Malayalees in Ceylon.[32]

Since Malayalees were employed mostly in the industrial and service sectors of the economy they became competitors to the Sinhala youths who invariably were unable to face the challenge from the enterprising Malayalee immigrants in the employment market. At the same time unemployment began to surface in the country with the Depression of the thirties. Apparently, the Sinhala feeling was that the influx of Malayalees was the main cause for the unemployment in Ceylon. In a memorandum submitted to a commission appointed in1927 for making constitutional reforms, a group of Ceylonese workmen expressed in clear terms their grievances against the immigration of Indian labourers in general and Malayalees in particular with the following words: "We feel very keenly the menace to Ceylonese labour occasioned by the influx of foreign and especially Malayalee labourers. Competition with such labour is scarcely possible for the workmen of this country, due chiefly to the low standard of living of such labourers".[33] The resentment against Malaylees reached its climax during the years following the Economic Depression of the thirties. Goonesinha, a prominent Sinhala leader openly accused in the Legislative Council that: "The root cause for unemployment is that we have hundreds of Malaylees coming here and depriving Ceylonese labourers of work and undercutting them".[34] Curiously, Malaylees were even accused of promoting leftist ideology and for spreading some diseases. Naturally the wrath of the anti-Indian feeling was directed particularly against Malayalee migrants. They were attacked and their establishments were looted on many occasions. As a result of the open hostility of the natives most of the Malayalees were compelled to return to India.

MIGRATION TO THE GULF COUNTRIES

A new fertile land for migration on a massive scale has dawned in the horizon during the later half of twentieth century. It is the oil producing countries of West Asia which began to attract a number of immigrant workers of different categories since the oil boom of 1970s. Expatriate labour from different countries of the world took advantage of the openings and sought better fortunes in the West Asian countries comprising United Arab Emirates, Oman, Bahrain, Kuwait, Saudi Arabia, Yemen and Qatar. This migration, known as Gulf migration had attracted hundreds of thousands of people from India. Emigration from India to the Gulf is by and large a Kerala phenomenon.

India had trade relations with various countries of the Middle East from ancient past dating back to the pre-Christian era. Merchants and sailors from Arab lands used to frequent south Indian ports like Cranganore, Quilon, Calicut and engaged in trade with India. Migration from Middle East countries also took place on different occasions and settlements of the Arabs, Jews and Persians sprang up in different places along the west coast of India. While the Jews and the Parsis fall entirely of West Asian origin, Syrian Christians and Mappilla Muslims of Kerala also claim ethnic connections with West Asian countries on a limited scale. Merchants from India also sailed to the Arab lands and exchanged Indian goods with the Egyptian, Greek, Roman, Phoenician and Arab merchants in the past. The Arab centres like Aden, Socotra etc. were the ultima thule of the Indian sailors during the ancient past. It is also believed that Indian sailors also opened colonies in Socotra, Al Uman and other trading centres of the Gulf region during the pre-Christian era.

The links with the Gulf countries were maintained even after the establishment of European hegemony in the Indian sub-continent. Haj Pilgrims from India used to congregate in the Arab lands inspite of the unfriendly attitude of the Europeans towards the Muslims. Merchants from India also engaged in the trade with the Arab lands when the Gulf countries like Aden, Oman, Bahrain etc. were brought under British colonial control.[35] Indian currency continued to remain as legal tender in those countries till 1959. Merchants like the Khojas and Memons, from the Indian sub-continent and even Hindu merchants from Kutch in Gujarat settled down in the Gulf region and engaged in trade. Some of the Muslim settlers from the Indian sub-continent were citizens of Oman. Even the Hindus could construct a temple in Oman, though they were persecuted on different occasions.

Migration of the modern period to the Gulf region had its beginnings though on a small scale, when oil companies were opened during the 1930s. The European companies which started oil mining in the Gulf region inducted educated Indians in the clerical, junior administrative and supervisory categories of occupations from the very beginning. The outbreak of the Second World War brought many Indians in the Gulf region in different capacities. In fact, the merchants from India formed an Indian Association in Dubai in 1941.[36] However, Indian migrants in the Gulf region were not many as Table 3.6 given below indicates.

Table 3.6: Number of Indians in Various Countries of the Middle East in 1947

Name of the Country	*Number of Indians*
Aden	5594
Bahrain	1138
Egypt	1000
Iran	2500
Iraq	650
Kuwait	1250
Muscat	1145
Jordan, Palestine Lebanon, Syria	500
Turkey	N.A.
Total	13777

Source: *C.Kondapi,* Indians Abroad 1834-1949 (*New Delhi, Indian Council of World Affairs, 1949*), p. 528.[37]

A good number of the migrants of Indian origin were stated to be descendants of the merhants from India who migrated much earlier. The bulk of the migrants were those who moved since the opening of the oil companies. It is reported that there were about 2000 Indians in the Kuwait Oil Company; 600 in the British Petroleum Company at Bahrain; 600 in the Anglo-Indian Oil Company at Abu Dhabi. Even in Saudi Arabia and Abu Dhabi, there were a good number of Indians in the oil companies.

Migration during the Post-Independence Period

There was practically no increase in the flow of migration to the Gulf till the beginning of the sixties. Nevertheless, the accumulation of wealth in the oil rich Gulf countries from the fifties was a potent factor which could attract immigrant workers in the years to come. A starting point was made, when some of the oil rich countries embarked on certain welfare projects meant to the benefit of the ordinary citizens from the increased inflow of oil revenue. The launching of those projects like desalination schemes, the electricity generation schemes etc. during the 1960s attracted a number of immigrant workers to the Gulf countries. Most of the migrant workers hailed from the other Arab countries like Egypt, Jordan, Syria, Iraq and Lebanon. Nevertheless, there was marginal increase in the volume of migration from India. The total volume of migration in the various Gulf countries seemed to have gone upto 40,000 by 1970-71.

A number of factors were at work, in converting the Gulf region into a promised land for expatriate workers from different parts of the world. Close on the heels of the oil boom of 1970s, the oil rich countries embarked on a massive industrialisation programme aimed at diversifying the economy on modern lines. The programmes called for large number of skilled, semi-skilled and even unskilled hands to carry on the work especially during the initial stages. The various welfare oriented programmes also called for the service of large number of educated persons including doctors, nurses, teachers etc. In the wake of the oil-boom, the nationals of the Gulf countries themselves developed some sort of a consumer oriented outlook. Such a change in the attitude necessitated the services of a large number of hands for the supply and servicing of sohpisticated consumer durables and also for domestic services.

The size of the national population of the oil producing Gulf countries was extremely small. Labour participation was also low, clustering around 23 per cent of the total population in almost all the oil-producing Gulf countries.[38] The skill formation of the indigenous labour force was also very low. They were not in a position to handle any of the sophisticated machines and equipments needed for the modernisation. Under such conditions, the Gulf countries had no alternative but to rely on expatriate labour for meeting those purposes.

The oil rich Gulf countries which were initially depending on expatriate labour from the oil poor Arab countries required much more hands than the Arab countries could supply. At the same time, some of the Arab countries like Saudi Arabia which were depending mainly on expatriate labour from other Arab countries changed their policy for political reasons. A large number of expatriate workers from Egypt was withdrawn towards the closing days of President Sadat's administration. Furthermore, the Arabs were not in a position to supply large number of hands at short notice. On the other hand, many of the labour recruiting agencies operating in India and also in Pakistan were ready to supply any number of hands at short notice. The workers from the Indian sub-continent were ready to work at slightly lower rate of wages than the the rates demanded and paid to the Arab labourers. The nearness of the Indian sub-continent to the Gulf region, the ethnic-cum-trade connection with the Gulf region, the knowledge of English language and the widespread unemployment in the country etc, were operating as push factors in sending streams of migrants from India. Last but not least, the Government of India also tacitly encouraged the emigration of workers to the oil rich Gulf countries.

No wonder, migration to the Gulf region, which was very moderate till then assumed the characteristics of an exodus from the seventies of twentieth century. The number of migrants from India increased to 214,000 according to an estimate made by the IMF in 1978.[39] The estimated number has gone upto 950,000 with the work participants among them totalling 599,500 in 1980-81.[40] The number of Indian migrants to the Gulf region seemed to have gone upto 1.7 million in 1983 and to about 2.8 million by 1990s.[41] The number of Indian emigrants in the Gulf region seems to have gone upto 3.07 million by 2000.[42]

Countries of Destination of the Migrants in the Gulf Region

Indian emigrants are to be found in almost all the labour importing countries of the Middle East. Prominent among them are Saudi Arabia, United Arab Emirates, Bahrain, Kuwait, Oman and Qatar. Indian emigrants are also found in Yemen, Iraq, Iran and Libya. Table 3.7 gives the size of Indian labourers in various Gulf countries as on 1981.

Table 3.7: Number of Indian Expatriate Workers in Various Gulf Countries in 1981

Sl. No.	Name of the Country	Number of Indian workers
1.	Saudi Arabia	80,000
2.	Kuwait	80,000
3.	United Arab Emirates	250,000
4.	Oman	65,000
5.	Libya	40,000
6.	Bahrain, Iraq and Qatar	75,000
7.	Yemen Arab Republic	5,000
8.	Jordan	3,500
9.	Yemen	1,000
	Total	599,500

Source: Stated in the Parliament by the Minister for External Affairs, Government of India in 1983.

Among the Gulf countries, United Arab Emirates comprising Abu Dhabi, Dubai, Sharjah and the poor village states of Ras Al Khaimah, Al-Qaiwan, Ajman and Fujairah have been depending on imported labour for a long period from various parts of the world. The estimated size of population of UAE in 1975 was 6.55 lakhs. Out of them non-nationals from different parts of the world totalled 4.55 lakhs.[43] The Indian component of the expatriate population was stated to be 1.07 lakhs in 1975.[44] As can be seen from the Table the size of the ex-patriate workers from India has increased to 2.5 lakhs by 1981. The number has been swelling further and by 2000 Indians in UAE seems to have gone upto 10 lakhs.[45] During the initial stages most of the Indians were employed in the construction sector. Subsequently Indians are employed in all occupations requiring better skill and technical competence.

Another important country which had attracted Indian workers is Bahrain. Prior to independence, it was a British Protectorate where Indian merchants had settled down and engaged in import and export trade. Indians used to arrive in the island as clerks, technicians and nurses from 1930s. Since 1970s, large numbers of Indian workers were engaged in construction work and as assistants in various banking and shipping companies.

Oman, another Sultanate had special connections with India during the British period. Indian business community from north west dominated the trade of Oman from the 19th century. During British days Indian civil servants manned various departments. Oman embarked on a construction programme after the ascendancy of the present Sultan who deposed his father as the ruler. Significantly, the Indians formed roughly 50 per cent of the expatriate population of Oman in 1975.[46] A good number of engineers, technicians and other categories of personnel from India are employed in Oman.

Kuwait is another country which has attracted large number of migrants from India. The national population of Kuwait was about 1.36 million in 1980. Expatriates from various countries constituted double the number of Kuwaiti labour force. The number of Indian migrants was comparatively less till 1975. The number swelled to 80,000 in 1981 mainly as a result of the withdrawal of Egyptian workers in Kuwait. The willingness of Indians to accept lower wages than those demanded by the Jordanians and Palestinians also accounts for the increase in the number of Indian workers. Indians are found in the professional, technical and also inferior categories of occupations in Kuwait. Most of the immigrants returned to India during the First Gulf War of 1991 . At the end of the war some of them came back to Kuwait and the size of the Indian population totalled 2.8 lakhs by 2000[47]

Saudi Arabia is another haven of migrants from India. Till 1975 majority of the expatriates in that country were of Arabic stock. Since then it has reversed its policy and accordingly the complexion of the migrants tilted in favour of non-Arabic stock. For political reasons, they prefer Asians for different categories of occupations. The number of Indian labour force has gone up from 15,000 in 1975 to nearly 80,000 by 1981. Since then, there has been a massive inflow from India. The number appears to have swelled to 12 lakhs by 2000.[48]

Qatar is another country which depends on immigrant labour. The local population which was estimated at 67,850 in 1975 against an immigrant population of 97,000.[49] Indian labour force in Qatar formed about 25,000. The number of Indian labour in 2000 is stated to be 1.2 lakhs.

Migration has also taken place in Yemen, Iraq, Iran and Libya. During the pre-independence period, Aden, the capital of Yemen was a place of attraction to Indian migrants who were mainly traders and service personnel. With the withdrawal of Britain from Yemen practically all the migrants left Aden. Iran and Iraq have also been centres of emigrants from India in the past. Migrants were mainly professional and other classes of educated persons. Since the outbreak of hostilities between the two countries majority of the migrants left both the countries. Libya, a country in the Mediterranean coast, has also emerged as a place of destination of a large number of expatriates from India.

Sectors of Employment in the Gulf Region

Migration to the Gulf as stated earlier, became a conspicuous phenomenon ever since the launching of the massive construction programmes and other attempts for creating a diversified industrial economy on modern lines by utilising the oil revenue. Different categories of workers were inducted from many countries. The expatriate workers employed in the Gulf can be classified as construction workers, employees of government and public sector institutions and personnel employed in private firms. In addition, there are businessmen, traders and domestic servants. The exact proportion of the workers under each of these categories is not known. During the mid-seventies, when Asian migration was in its infancy it was stated that over one third of the expatriate workers worked in construction sector, 24 per cent in the services, 15 per cent in trade and 9 per cent in agriculture.[50] Since then, there would have been a sea change as the bulk of the Asian migrants arrived after that date. Evidently,the Indian migrants would be employed in all these sectors.

Construction sector would be the largest sector where Indians are employed. Indian workers are employed in all types of occcupations like those of the unskilled workers, skilled craftsmen, civil engineers and managers in the construction sector. The construction companies are owned by the American, British, Cypriot, Arab, Korean and even Indian entrepreneurs.

A large number of Indians are employed in different occupations under government departments. Special mention may be made of the large number of doctors and nurses employed in the Gulf region. Significantly, the bulk of the nurses hail from Kerala.

The Gulf region as stated earlier, began to attract migrants from India when British and American companies started oil drilling from the thirties. Many of them are still employed even now in such companies. Similarly, many private companies and firms which engage in industrial and business activities engage Indians in different occupations.

As stated earlier, merchants were the first to migrate from India. Even now they engage in various business activities. Apart from the old historical trade links with the African ports, Indian merchants have recently opened Middle East trade with Europe and Africa. They also carry on trade with India and the Gulf countries. Within the Gulf countries, they own small shops, departmental stores and restaurants in the cities like Kuwait, Manama, Dubai, Abu Dhabi, Muscat and Mulrah.[51]

Though not numerically large, they are very influential particularly in Dubai, Abu Dhabi and Oman.

Domestic sector constitutes another avenue for employment in the Gulf. Large number of Indians are employed as cooks, sweepers, housekeepers, gardeners and *ayahs*. Many of the unskilled illegal migrants engage in such categories of occupation. Though the government of India has banned the emigration of women for domestic service, many of them manage to reach the Gulf countries through the connivance or tacit approval of the emigration authorities. Myron Weiner describes in graphic terms the presence of Indian ayahs with the following words: "The *ayahs* are a particularly conspicuous part of the local scene, in several Gulf states. In Kuwait, for example, a thousand or more Indian *ayahs* can be seen on Sunday evening in front of the city's Catholic Church, talking, strolling with one another and with young Indian babies".[52] The bulk of the *ayahs* are stated to be from Goa.

Though the workers are distributed among different sectors, they may be holding different occupations on the basis of their qualifications and experience. In the construction sector, for example, while a few were employed as engineers, the majority were mere skilled or even unskilled labourers. Occupational distribution of the workers provides a rough idea on the quality of the workers. On the whole, the workers in the Gulf region were employed in occupations requiring less professional skill and qualification, than their counterparts in other parts of the world. While migrants to the developed nations included the families and dependants, the migrants to the Gulf consisted mostly of the workers unaccompanied by their dependents.

States of Origin of the Migrants and Their Socio-economic Background

Most of the migrants hailed from Kerala, Andhra Pradesh, Punjab, Gujarat, Goa, Maharashtra, Tamil Nadu and so on from the very beginning. Of the seven states, Kerala is supposed to send the largest numbers, approximately about half the total from India. The ethnic-cum-trade connections which Kerala had with the Middle East countries and the mounting pressure of unemployment would have accounted for the emigration of the large contingent of migrants from Kerala. However, no accurate data on the quantum of emigration are available in respect of any other state. According to a survey conducted by the Government of Kerala, there were 1.86 lakh migrants in the Gulf region from Kerala in 1980.[53] Other sources which contend the official figure to be an underestimate provide an altogether different figure on the volume of migration from Kerala. According to one of such sources, the total number of migrant workers would have been 3.5 lakhs in 1981.[54] According to Zachariah the size of migrants from Kerala in the Gulf region has gone to 13.61 lakhs by 1999.[55]

Migrants to the Gulf as stated earlier, are employed in the construction sector, government service and also in domestic work. The exact occupational position of the migrants in these sectors depend on their educational qualifications. While some of the occupations call for specialisation of a high order, a good many of them may require only low level of technical skill and experience. At the same time, some of the occupations like construction, or trade or service can carry on even without any education or with a moderate level of general education. The size of the migrants holding different categories of occupations under each sector in turn depends on the proportion of people holding different levels of education. However, practically no information regarding the educational profile of the migrants is available. The only data available are certain surveys and micro-level studies conducted in Kerala. They shed light on the educational profile of the migrants as Table 3.8 indicates.

Table 3.8: Educational Qualification of the Migrants from Kerala

Sl. No.	*Level of Education*	*Percentate of Migrants*
1.	Below Secondary (Unskilled)	48.9
2.	Below Secondary (Skilled)	20.76
3.	Secondary (Unskilled)	13.2
4.	Secondary (Skilled)	11.5
5.	Degree (General)	4.6
6.	Degree (Technical)	1.5
	Total	100.0

Source: G.O.K. *Housing and Employment Survey 1980*, (Trivandrum, Directorate of Economics and Statistics, 1980). p. 47

Nearly half the number of migrants fall under the category of people possessing educational qualification below the Secondary School level. Some of them can be illiterates or literates with no formal education at all. Mention may be made in this connection that the literates with primary level of education formed 47.6 per cent and illiterates 6.6 per cent of the total migrants according to another survey.[56] Degree holders and technically qualified professionals were not many. Naturally, the overwhelming majority of the migrants would be holding inferior categories of occupations. Since then, the educational profile of the migrants have underegone sea change. In fact, the UAE government has banned the entry of unskilled workers in 1999.[57]

Conditions of Employment

Wage rates of the migrants to the Gulf region vary from country to country. The rates are the highest in Saudi Arabia, Kuwait and United Arab Emirates. It is the lowest in Oman where the rates are stated to be just one half of those of Kuwait or Saudi Arabia. There is no uniform rate of wages for the same type of work. Discrimination of wage rates was a regular phenomenon. On the whole, wages offered to Indian migrants have been much lower than those offered to the Arab nationals and the nationals from Europe. Indians as well as nationals from Korea and Bangladesh have been willing to accept wages much below the normal rates. Nevertheless, the wage rates are much higher than those prevailing in India.

Notwithstanding the fairly attracative rates of wages, workers from India and also from other Asian countries suffer from many disabilities. They do not have any political right. They cannot own property, engage in their own trade without a partner from the Gulf country or organise trade unions. Social security arrangements are yet to take firm roots in the Gulf countries. The working conditions and even the payment of the full salary in terms of the agreement depend to a large extent on the honesty and integrity of the employers. The migrants cannot agitate against overwork or denial of overtime allowances or inadequate provision of accommodation for subsidised food.

They do not have even accessibility to the social life of the nationals of the Gulf countries. They have to organise their own enclaves for social life, sports clubs, schools, literary and debating societies. Though some of the expatriates were housed in separate enclaves, migrants from Kerala are not housed in separate enclaves nor are they totally isolated from the social life of the countries. Some of them have engaged in trade as partners with the Arab nationals.

Remittance of Money from the Gulf

One of the main attractions for the nationals of different countries including India to migrate to the Gulf region appears to be the prospects of remitting money to their home countries. Though the cost of living is fairly high in the Gulf countries, the scope for sending money is very bright for various reasons. First, the salaries the migrants receive in the

Gulf countries are fairly high in comparison to the salary rates prevailing in India. Second, the Gulf countries do not impose any restrictions on the remittance of money to foreign countries. Third, the absence of costly entertainment facilities, gambling etc., in combination with cheap price for consumer durables and petrol, compel the migrants to save a good portion of their income. Accommodation is invariably provided by the employer and many items of food are subsidised. Naturally, the prospects for saving a good proportion of their earning are also bright. Since the duration of service in the Gulf region is invariably for a short period, the migrants have to save a portion of their earnings in order to survive and make a living at a later date.

Further, the migration to the Gulf region is by and large a male phenomenon in which most of the female members are left at home. As a result, the migrants are compelled to send at least a portion of their earnings for the maintenance of their kith and kin at home. In contrast to this, the migrants to the U.K., the West European countries and America are allowed to take their families also to the places of destination. Most of them have a fair chance for settling down in those countries. Needless to say, migrants invest part of their savings in those Western countries. On the other hand, migration to the Gulf does not provide much scope for investment by the expatriate workers. The result is remittance of fairly large sums of money from the Gulf region ever since migration started to the Gulf.

Though, the migrants used to send money to India, the volume involved was not big during the earlier periods of migration. There was however, a substantial increase in the quantum of remittances since the mid-seventies of twentieth century. However, no accurate data on the inflow of remittances from the Gulf are available. The inflow of money from the Gulf region arrives mainly through private remittances. The main source of private transfer was the Sterling area in which most of the Gulf countries are included. The remittances through private transfer were not much in the past. With the outflow of large number of migrants to the Gulf from the seventies, private transfer from the Sterling area began to swell. Apparently, the inflow would be from the Gulf region. Even then, private transfer from the Gulf region can at the most provide only a rough picture of the inflow of remittances because Saudi Arabia where a large number of migrants works, is not in the Sterling area. Further, there used to be large inflow of *Kuzhalpanam* or illegal transfer from foreign countries. In the absence of other sources the increased volume of inflow should be construed as those that are remitted by the expatriates (see Table 3.9).

Table 3.9: Private Transfer Payment Since 1960-61

Year	*Receipts under Private (Rs. In million)*	*Transfer Payments Receipts under Private Transfer Payment from Sterling Area (Rs. In million)*
1960-61	449	320
1970-71	1364	372
1971-72	1622	571
1972-73	1653	458
1973-74	2033	763
1974-75	2799	1108
1975-76	5412	2481
1976-77	7457	3452
1977-78	10293	6157
1978-79	10593	6075
1979-80	16320	9784
1980-81	22668	15286
1981-82	22371	13169
1982-83	25410	14961
1983-84	27851	14759
1984-85	31162	25257
1987-88	34984	16773
1989-90	37977	15628
1991-92	94189	35406
1993-94	114964	59443
1996-97	439680	152470

Source: Reserve Bank of India, *Report on Currency and Finance*, Various years.

As can be seen from the Table, there was marked increase in the volume of private transfer payments since the seventies of 20th century. The rate of increase from the Sterling area was much more than the overall increase. While the overall increase recorded a percentage of 6940 for the period 1960-61 to 1984-85, the percentage of increase from the Sterling area was 7892. Apparently, much of the increase could be attributed to the increased flow of receipts from the Gulf area.

Since the expatriate workers from Kerala form the largest contingent from India, a major share of the remittances from the Gulf would be flowing to Kerala. However, neither the Reserve Bank of India, nor any other official agency maintains any account about the inflow of remittances to any particular state. Naturally, one has to rely on the estimates and findings of private researchers. According to Deepak Lal, the receipts from the Gulf region accounted for about 25 per cent of the state domestic product during 1980s.[58] In his study on Gulf migration,

Zachariah estimated inward remittances from the Gulf region at Rs.3530 crores for the year 1998.[59] It would account only for about 10 per cent of the state domestic product. On the other hand, another authority, estimated the inflow at 20 per cent of the state domestic product since 1990s.[60] Notwithstanding the wide variations about the volume of remittances, it is a well known fact that Kerala has been receiving a fairly large amount of money from the Gulf region since the oil boom of the seventies of the last century. Needless to say, Kerala economy has been undergoing a sea change since the inward remittances from the Gulf started to flow. Since independence the per capita income in Kerala has been lower than that of the all India level. However, the per capita income of Kerala began to rise above the all-India level from 1993-94.[61] Apparently, it would be due to the inflow funds from the Gulf. Similarly, such conditions of prosperity like the improvement in the standard of living, reduction of the incidence of poverty, the construction boom etc. discernible in Kerala are all due directly or indirectly to the inflow of remittances.

In brief, most of the migrants are sojourners who are bound to return to Kerala. Naturally, they retain their links with Kerala in various forms. In spite of the temporary nature of their stay they associate themselves by organizing Malayalee Associations and Kerala Samajams. These organizations serve primarily as networks which facilitate the ongoing process of migration and as self help unions. Performance of various cultural programmes, celebrations of festivals like Onam etc. are some of the important activities of these organizations. Malayalees of different walks of life attend such functions. Through these cultural performances the expatriate Malayalees in the Gulf strive to maintain their identity. Some Christian sects maintain their separate identities by establishing their own separate places of worship.

Migration to the U.S.

Apart from the Gulf region the USA has turned out to be the most important destination of the migrants from India since 1965. As already stated, migrants were not welcome to the USA during the early decades of 20th century. Emigration was on an insignificant scale even during the post-Second World War period. Indians were allowed to become naturalised Americans only in 1946, but the law which provided for naturalisation also imposed a quota restriction of 100 persons of Indian origin per year. Dilip Singh Saund who became a Congressman in 1956 in the U.S., was one of the earliest Indians to become a naturalized

American.[62] The number of East Indians, a term used to refer to the immigrants from India in those days, admitted to the U.S. between 1946-1965 was stated to be around 6500. Immigration of those with professional and technical qualifications was liberalized through another legislation in 1965. Since then, there was a steady increase in the number of immigrants to the U.S. According to the 1990 census the total strength of Indian population in the U.S. was 814000.[63] It went up to 1.6 million by 2000. The concentration of Indians are in California, New Jersey, New York, Chicago and so on.

Most of the Indians are employed in the professional and technical fields. During 1980s "more than two-fifths of male professionals were engineers and over a quarter physians. Among female professionals better than three-fifths were in the health-diagnosing occupations".[64] Of late,business activities undertaken by the Indians are also on the increase. Interestingly, the Indians of Gujarati origin own a large number of hotels and petrol bunks in the east coast of the U.S. With the increase in the number of emigrants from India to the U.S., inward remittances from there appears to be increasing. The spurt in the inflow of private transfer payments from the Dollar currency area is a clear indicator of such a possibility. In 1980s, when the size of Indian immigrants in the U.S. was not big, private transfer payments from the Dollar currency area accounted for hardly one fifth of the total. However, by 1996-97, it accounted for nearly half of the total private transfer payments. In absolute terms, inward remittances from the Dollar currency area amounted to only Rs. 594 crores in 1984-85. It went on increasing and by 1996-97, upto which only separate figures are available, the private transfer payments from the Dollar currency area went upto Rs.22,539 crores.[65] Needless to say, the size of immigrants from India was also increasing during the same period.

Migration of Keralites was practically nil till the attainment of independence. Infact, the entry of Malayalees to the U.S. dates to the post independence period. One Fr. Chiramell, who was murdered by some assailants, is believed to be the first person from Kerala to migrate to the U.S. Since then, a few doctors and priests reached the U.S. One notable migrant was Fr. Mathew Thekkekara, a Catholic priest from Changanacherry who reached the U.S. in 1952. His credentials as a scientist was well recognised and he became a senior scientist of NASA. Another earlier migrant was Dr. Sreedharan Nair.[66]

Migration from Kerala gained momentum with the liberalization of entry restrictions in 1965. Since then, some sort of a brain drain ensued by which well-educated youngsters whose ranks were swelling and who were not getting suitable employment in Kerala started to move in large numbers. The estimated size of Malayalee population in the USA was around 35,000 in 1980. They formed roughly 10 per cent of the Indian population of 387225 in 1980.[67] If the same trend continues, Keralites in the U.S. would be more than 1.5 lakhs in 2000.

The Kerala immigrants in the U.S. are better educated in comparison with any other immigrant group. During 1980s about 94 per cent of the Keralites were educated upto the secondary stage and 55 per cent upto the college level. Those with professional qualifications are equally high. Among them, medical doctors form 10.5 per cent, engineers 10 per cent, educators 7 per cent, researchers and scientists 5 per cent, nurses and para-medical professionals 30 per cent.[68] Compared to the migrants to the Gulf region, educational profile of the migrants to the U.S. is far superior. The level of earnings of Keralites are even higher than those of the average Americans. Since qualified professionals alone are able to get through the sifting process of immigration, the majority of the Keralites fall within the category of middle and upper classes of American standards.[69] Some of them like Dr. Zachariah, Shasi Tharoor, Dr. Vinod Thomas etc., could make a name in the U.S.

Malayalees in the U.S. have formed their own associations in various parts of America. They celebrate Onam and other days of importance in Kerala. Various cultural programmes are performed under the auspices of their associations. The Syrian Christians belonging to various denominations have set up their own places of worship and even eccelesiastic institutions in the U.S. Thus the Malayalees in the U.S. strive to maintain their identity and to preserve their links with their native land by establishing their associations and religious institutions.

Migration to the U.K.

Though India was directly under the British administration for nearly two centuries there was very little migration to Great Britain during the pre-Independence period. The imperial tone and racial prejudices of the Britishers stood in the way for any kind of migration from India. As already stated, a few students and businessmen were the only people who migrated to Great Britain in the first instance. During the early decades of twentieth century a few professionals were added. Migration to U.K. received a boost with the induction of some Sikh soldiers for service in the country. However, Indians formed an insignifcant section of the population at the time of Independence. The real beginnings of migration to the U.K. can be stated to have started with the arrival of ethnic Indians from West Indies during the fifties of 20th century. A few Punjabi workers of different categories also migrated to Great Britain in the wake of the labour shortage experienced during the post-War period.[70] When the British colonies like Kenya, Tanzania and Uganda attained independence a good number of ethnic Indians who had settled there earlier were compelled to migrate to the U.K. because of the hostile attitude of the natives towards ethnic Indians. The compulsory expulsion of ethnic Indians during the regime of Idi Amin in Uganda is a well known fact. Subsequently, migration of a large number of professionals also ensued. The ethnic Indians comprising West Indians from the Caribbean island, the East Indians from the east African countries and native Indians totalled 779,900 in 1989.[71] By 2001, the Indian population numbered 10,54,00 which accounted for about 1.8 per cent of the population of U.K. The migrants on their part opened Indian food and cloth shops in the places of settlement. *Gurudwaras*, *mandirs* and *masjids* were also established in many places.[72]

Majority of the Indian migrants in U.K. are professionals of different categories of whom those with the medical and allied professions form an important group. There are a good number of factory hands and technicians of different trades. The occupational profile of the Indians compare favourably with the native population. The average earnings of Indians are even higher than those of the natives. According to an author, the ethnic Indians face a Jewish future in U.K. apparently because of their prosperity.[73] Some Indian businessmen like Swaraj Paul, Luxmi Mittal have become very rich people.

Malayalees, as mentioned earlier were later entrants to the U.K. Those who migrated during the initial stages were students. A notable migrant to U.K. before the independence of India was V.K. Krishna Menon who became a Cabinet Minister in free India. He founded the India League and fought for India's freedom during the pre-independence period. Malaylee migrants in the medical field have become a significant segment among the ethnic settlers in U.K.

Migration to Other Countries

Another country which attracts migrants on a moderate scale is Canada. As already stated, migration to Canada was not a smooth affair during the initial stages. Till the end of the Second World War, most of the migrants were unskilled workers. Since then large number of skilled workers and professionals began to flock to Canada. While the earlier migrants were Sikhs from the Punjab, later on migrants from other parts of India also joined the stream. The migrants from India who totalled 173645 in 1991 constituted 4 per cent of all the immigrants in Canada. Nearly 26 per cent of the Indian immigrants in Canada had University education, a percentage higher than the overall average in Canada. Similarly, the per capita income of the immigrants from India was much higher than that of the country as a whole.[74]

Keralites form a considerable section of the immigrants from India. However, data on the magnitude of the immigrants from Kerala are scanty. According to a survey made by the Department of Economics and Statistics, Government of Kerala, the migrants from Kerala numbered only 4115 in 1998. There would certainly be more number of Keralites occupying different jobs in Canada.[75]

European countries like Germany and Italy have also attracted a fairly large number of Keralites during the post-Independence period. According to a survey conducted by the Government of Kerala, there were 11,502 persons from Kerala employed in various European countries in 1998.[76] Most of them are in the medical profession either as doctors or nurses or technicians. Another country which attracts immigrants from India is Australia. The White Australia policy was cancelled at the end of the Second World War and at present Australia admits non-whites including Indians. Most of the Indians are professionals. Immigrant Malayalees also fall under this catetory.

Migration on a fairly large scale had taken place from Indian sub-continent to the African countries like South Africa, Kenya, Uganda etc., during the latter half of the nineteenth century. Among the migrants from India, those from Kerala region were practically nil except a few in Kenya. They were employed mostly in the railways, schools, medical and civil services. However, most of them have moved either to the United Kingdom or Australia in course of time. With the end of Aparthied a few Keralites have migrated to South Africa. Nigeria and Ethiopia also turned out to be countries of immigration from Kerala. Most of them were in the teaching profession. However, with the eruption of political instability in those countries most of the migrants have returned to India or moved to other countries. A few Keralites comprising teachers, doctors and professionals have settled down in Botswana. According to a survey made by the Government of Kerala, there were 3388 Keralites employed in various African countries in 1980.[77]

Migration on a small scale has taken place in Indonesia during the pre-independence period. Most of the migrants were Muslims from Gujarat, Tamil Nadu and Kerala. Majority of the Muslim immigrants from Malabar region of Kerala have got absorbed in the Indonesian society by marrying Indonesian women.[78] Curiously, many of them regarded themselves as "Malabar Pakistanis" soon after India's independence and some of them in turn landed in trouble. Nevertheless, all of them seem to entertain sweet memories about Kerala. Interestingly, the Malayalam novelist S.K. Pottekkat, in one of his travelogues has given a vivid description of how he happened to visit one "Malabar-Pakistani restaurant" owned by one Malabari Muslim in Indonesia and the hospitality extended to him by the Mappilla immigrants during his travel in that country.[79]

Malayalees had also set foot in Japan soon after the first World War. One of the interesting migrants from Travancore was A.M. Nair who reached Japan in 1928 for the purpose of education. Subsequently, he married a Japanese woman and settled down in Japan. Known as Nair San, he became a leading businessman in Japan.[80] However, very few Malayalees could migrate to Japan apparently on account of the restrictions on immigration imposed by the Japanese government.

Indian ethnic communities of fairly large numbers are found in Mauritius, Trinidad, Fiji, Guiana. South Africa and so on. As already stated, fairly large number of people from India migrated to these countries, mostly under the indenture system during the early stages of migration. Most of the ethnic Indians found in those countries are the descendents of those migrants who opted to settle down there. They are mainly Hindi speaking people who are well entrenched in those countries, though they encounter opposition from the local people in countries like Fiji. Malayalee element among them is practically nil.

Conclusion

From that of a handful Malayalam speaking people migrating to the nearby countries like Burma (Myanmar), Sri Lanka or Malaysia at the beginning of 20th century, migratory movements of Malayalees have acquired the characteristic of a stream towards the close of 20th century. Hundreds of thousands of Malayalees seek their fortunes in foreign lands like the Gulf countries and the United States of America during that period. Though not in large numbers, Malayalees are also present in many other parts of the world like the Great Britain, Canada, Western Europe, Australia, Malaysia and so on. The diasporic Malayalees in turn have organized Malayalee Associations and Kerala Samajams in all those places where they have settled down. Some of them particularly the various Syrian Christian sects have even established their own places of worship and ecclesiastic institutions in those distant lands. These organizations and institutions serve them as networks for consolidating their hold in those foreign lands and also as mechanism for maintaining their identity. The ranks of the expatriate Malayalees include politicians, administrators, executives, doctors, engineers, scientists, artists, salesmen, technicians, nurses, and ordinary workers. They have been able to maintain high standards of efficiency and professional competence in all places where they have set foot. No wonder, they could bring name and fame to Kerala, the narrow strip of land located in the south western corner of India.

Notes and References

1. Shirras, Findlay: "Indian Migration" in Walter F. Willcox (ed.) *International Migration, Vol.II Interpretation* (New York, Gorden and Breach Science Publishers, 1969), p. 596.
2. Shirras, Findlay, *op.cit.*, p. 592.
3. Chakravarti, N.R., *Indian Minority in Burma* (Oxford University Press, 1971), p. 15.
4. Chakravarti, N.R., *op.cit.*, p. 56.
5. Chakravarti, N.R., *op.cit.*, p. 22.
6. Uma Sankar Singh, "Indians in Burma" in I.J. Bahadur Singh (ed.) *Indians in South East Asia* (New Delhi, Sterling Publishers, 1982), p. 100.
7. Chakravarti, N.R., *op.cit.*, pp. 169-72.
8. Chakravarti, N.R., *op.cit.*, p. 30.
9. *Census of India 1931, Vol.II, Imperial Tables, Table XV Languages.*
10. *Census of India 1921, Imperial Tables.*
11. Mayer Adrian: *Land and Society in Malabar* (Bombay, Oxford University Press, 1952), p. 175.
12. *Census of Travancore 1921*. Part I, p. 27.
13. *Census of India, 1931, Imperial Tables.*
14. Kernial Singh Sandhu: *Indians in Malaya Immigrations and Settlement 1786-1957* (Cambridge, at the University Press, 1969), p. 47.
15. Kernial Singh Sandhu: *op.cit*, p. 56.
16. Kernial Singh Sandhu: *op.cit*, p. 68.
17. Kernial Singh Sandhu: *op.cit*, p. 70.
18. R.Raju: "Indians in Peninsular Malaya' in I.J. Bahadur Singh (ed.) *Indians in South East Asia* (New Delhi, Sterling Publishers, 1982), p. 54.
19. Kernial Singh Sandhu: *op.cit*, p. 54.
20. Raju Kurian: *Patterns of Migration from Kerala* (Trivandrum, M.Phi. Dissertation, CDS, 1976), p. 40.
21. Raju Kurien, *op.cit.*, p. 23.
22. A.K. Gopalan, *In the Cause of the People: Reminiscences* (Delhi, Orient Longman, 1973), p. 126.
23. Raju Kurien, *op.cit.*, p.
24. *Census of India 1931, Cochin,.Part I, Special Migration Table.*
25. Census of the Princely State of Travancore 1931, *Part I Report, Special Emigration Table.*

26. *Census of India 1931*, Madras, Part I Report, p. 84.
27. *Ibid.*
28. Kondapi, C. *Indian's Overseas* (Oxford University Press, 1951), p. 327.
29. *Census of India 1921*, Vol.XXV, Travancore, Part I Report (Trivandrum, Government Press 1922), p. 28.
30. *Census of India, Cochin* 1931 Part I Report, *Special Emigration Table.*
31. Gopalan, A.K. *In the Cause of the People Reminiscences* (Bombay, Orient Longman 1973), p. 120.
32. Gopalan, A.K., *op.cit.*, p. 29.
33. Wikramasinghe, Nira, quotes from "Nathan MSS 619 Special Circulation No.291, Memorandum from Ceylon Workers" in Migration and the Otherness in Sri Lanka" Crispin Bates et.al. *Community Empire and Migration:South Asians in Diaspora* (Palmgrave, New York, 2001), p. 173.
34. Wikramasinghe, Nira, quotes from CO 54/907/10, Strike Bulletin Special, 11, April 1931 (See Wikramasinghe, Nira, op.cit., p. 175).
35. Mana Saud Al Otiba: *Petroleum and the Economy of the United Arab Emirates* (London, Croom Helm 1977), p. 120.
36. Weiner, Myron: "International Migration and Development: Indians in the Persian Gulf" in *Population and Development Review*, Vol.8, No.1, March 1982.
37. C. Kondapi, *op.cit.*, p. 528.
38. J.S. Birks and C.A. Sinclair, *Arab Manpower: The Crisis of Development* (New York, St.Martins Press, 1980), p. 16.
39. *IMF Survey 1978*, September 1978.
40. M.C. Madhavan, "Dimensions of Indian Emigration", *The Hindu*, February 1985.
41. B.A. Prakash, "Gulf Migration and its Economic Impact" in *Economic and Political Weekly*, December 12, 1998.
42. The estimated size of Indian immigrants in various Gulf countries as on February 2000 has been as given below:

Country	No. of Indians in lakhs
Saudi Arabia	12
UAE	10
Oman	3.4
Kuwait	2.8
Bahrain	1.3
Qatar	1.2
Total	30.7

Source : Gulf Division of External Affairs, New Delhi; quoted by K.C. Zachariah et.al. in *Kerala's Gulf Connection* (Trivandrum, Centre for Development Studies, 2002) p. 142.

43. J.S. Birks and C.A. Sinclair, "International Migration Project: An Enquiry into the Middle East Labour Market" in *International Migration Review*, Vol.IXIII, Spring 1979.

44. Deepak Nayyar, "International Labour Migration from India: A Macro Economic Analysis" in Rashid Amjad (ed.) *To the Gulf and Back* (New Delhi, I.L.O. Asian Employement Programme, 1989).
45. Ministry of External Affairs, *op.cit.*
46. J.S. Birks and C.A.Sinclair, *op.cit.*
47. Ministry of External Affairs, *op.cit.*
48. *Ibid.*
49. J.S. Birks and C.A. Sinclair, *op.cit.*
50. Ismail Serageldin and James Sockart, "Migration and Manpower Needs in the Middle East and North Africa 1975-85" in *Finance and Development*, December 1980.
51. Weiner Myron, *op.cit.*
52. Weiner Myron, *op.cit.*
53. G.O.K. *Housing and Employment Survey, 1980* (Trivandrum, Department of Economics and Statistics).
54. Ibrahim P., "Impact of West Asian Remittances on the Economy of Kerala" in *Journal of Kerala Studies*.
55. K.C. Zachariah et.al., *Kerala's Gulf Connection* (Trivandrum, Centre for Development Studies, 2002), p. 143.
56. P.R. Gopinathan Nair, *Report of a Survey of Returned Migrants (Summary)*, Trivandrum, Centre for Development Studies, Mimeo, Unpublished.
57. K.C. Zachariah, *op.cit.* p. 160
58. Deepak Nayyar, "International Labour Migration from India: A Macro Economic Analysis" in Rashid Amjad (ed.) *To the Gulf and Back* (New Delhi, I.L.O. Asian Employment Programme, 1989), p. 120.
59. K.C. Zachariah, E.T. Mathew and S. Irudaya Rajan: "Consequences of Migration: Socio-Economic and Demographic Dimensions in K.C. Zachariah (ed.) *Kerala's Gulf Connections* (Trivandrum, Centre for Development Studies, 2002) p. 64.
60. K.P. Kannan and K.S. Hari: "Kerala's Gulf Connections: Remittances and Their Macro-economic Impact", in K.C. Zachariah et.al. *Kerala's Gulf Connection* (Trivandrum, CDS, 2002), p. 211.
61. In 1980-81 the per capita domestic product of Kerala was only Rs.1463/- against the all India level of Rs.1627/-. The per capita product continued to be lower than that of the all India level throughout 1990s. Since 1993-94, onwards the per capita domestic product of Kerala was higher than the all India level (See Statistics for Planning 1993 and Statistics for Planning 2001, Trivandrum, Department of Economics, Government of Kerala).
62. Daniels, Roger: "Indian Diaspora in the United States" in Judith Brown (ed.) *Migration, the Asian Experience* (Oxford, St. Martin's Press 1994), p. 94.
63. Daniels, Roger, *op.cit.*, p. 95.
64. Daniels, Roger, *op.cit.*, p. 97.
65. Reserve Bank of India: *Report on Currency and Finance* (Various years.)
66. Dr. Paul P. Louis, "Early Immigrants" in K.P. Andrews (ed.) *Keralites in America: Community Reference Book* (New York, Literary Market Review 1983), pp. 106-107.

67. Andrews K.P., "Keralites in America: An Introduction" in K.P. Andrews (ed.), *op.cit.*, (New York, Literary Market Review, 1983), p. 99.
68. *Ibid.*
69. Karoor, Isaac; "History of Keralite: Immigration in United States" in K.P. Andrews (ed.) *Keralites in America, op.cit.*, pp. 102-103.
70. Helweg, Arthur W., "Indians in England: A Study of the International Relationships of Sending, Receiving and Migrant Societies" in M.S.A. Rao (ed.) *Studies on Migration* (New Delhi, Manohar 1986), p. 366.
71. Ceri Peach, "Three Phases of South Asian Emigration" in Judith Brown and Rosemary Foot (ed.) *Migration: The Asian Experience* (Oxford, St Martin's Press, 1994), p. 50.
72. Chandan Amarjit, *Indians in Britain* (New Delhi, Sterling Publishers Pvt. Ltd., 1986), p.32.
73. Ceri, Peach, *op.cit.*, p.50.
74. Surjit Singh: "Indian Immigration to Canada" in *Indian Journal of Labour Economics*, vol. 44, No. 4, Oct.-Dec. 1998.
75. Govt. of Kerala, *Report on the Activity Status of the Migrants and Returnees* (Trivandrum, Department of Economics and Statistics, 2000).
76. Govt. of Kerala, *op.cit.*
77. Govt. of Kerala, *Report of the Housing and Employment Survey* 1980 (Trivandrum, Dept. of Economics and Statistics, 1983).
78. B.D. Arora, "Indians in Indonesia" in I.J. Bahadur Singh (ed.) *Indians in South East Asia* (New Delhi, Sterling Publishers, 1982), pp. 120-126.
79. S.K. Pottekkatt; *Indonesian Diary, Vol.II* (Mal.) (Kottayam, National Book Stall, 1955).
80. A.M. Nair; *Nair San Jappanil Anpathi Anchu Varsham* (Malayalam); (Autobiography of A.M. Nair, Kottayam, D.C. Books, 1982).

Chapter 4

Trends in Internal Migration Since 1920

As already stated, hundreds of thousands of persons moved from India to distant lands from the early decades of nineteenth century inspite of the constraints to any form of mobility. However, the migratory movement thus started was essentially a state sponsored labour migration. Certain developments like the spread of education, growth of transport and communication, social awakening etc. which could weaken the constraints were underway since the middle of nineteenth century. Eventually different patterns of migration began to appear from the closing decades of nineteenth century. They were able to gain momentum during the years following the First World War in regions like Kerala. The main trends in the internal migration since 1920s would be delineated in the sections that follow.

Trends in the Intensity of Migration during the Pre-independence Period

Though migratory movement had its beginning in the early decades of twentieth century, it was not able to gain momentum in the country as a whole in the immediate future. In fact, it became sluggish, if not negative during the thirties. Table 4.1 indicates the total volume of outmigration in India as a whole, and the percentage of the same as a ratio to the total population.

Notwithstanding the marginal increase in the volume of outmigration in the country as a whole, the ratio of outmigration as a percentage to the total population in the country revolved around 2.50. Infact, there was a fall in the percentage of outmigrants from 2.59 in 1921 to 2.53 in 1931. In this connection the questions are: (i)Why there was a setback and (ii) why migration did not gather momentum inspite of the weakening of the constraints?

Basically, the pull factors were not sufficiently strong as to accelerate the rate of migration. Normally, people would be ready to migrate to

Table 4.1: Volume of Decennial Outmigration in India

Year	*Total Population*	*Total volume of the migrants*	*Percentage of the volume of migrants to the population*
1901	294361000	6247830	2.12
1911	315156000	8010241	2.54
1921	318942000	8270868	2.59
1931	352838000	8935693	2.53

Source: K.C.Zachariah, *A Historical Study of Intenal Migration in Indian Sub-Continent 1901-1931* (Bombay, Asia Publishing House, 1964).

another locality if the possibility for improving one's economic prospects are bright. Enough possibilities potentially capable of attracting large number of people were not forthcoming in many parts of India. At the same time, the constraints were still powerful inspite of various developments. Further, the linguistic and cultural barriers were so deep-rooted as to retard the movement of people from one state to another. Nevertheless, it was the subsequent developments which actually influenced the migratory movement in one way or other since the twenties. The beginnings of the migratory movements were made with the overall development of the economy which ushered in since the dawn of the twentieth century. The boom conditions which appeared during the First World War was conducive to the movement of people. However, some of the developments which ensued subsequently were not at all conducive to the migratory movement of people. The increasing tempo of competition in the foreign markets made the conditions precarious in the case of almost all industries which were thriving during the War period. Industries like the cotton textiles, sugar, iron and steel etc, were able to withstand the stiff competition soley because of the protection granted by the government. Needless to say, such developments could not naturally promote migration.

The economic depression of the thirties was another development which adversely affected the scope for migration. As a matter of fact, almost all the economic activities were adversely affected by the depression. It has been estimated for example, that the value of the principal crops fell from Rs. 1018 crores in 1929 to Rs. 534 crores in 1933.[1] Similarly, the export earnings of the country which stood at Rs. 345.5 crores in 1928-29 declined to Rs. 230.5 crores in 1930-31 and contined to fall further.[2] The country experienced some sort of a cash famine and to tide over the difficulties some of the industrial units were shut down. Large number of workers from various factories like the jute, collieries, printing press were retrenched. The number of labourers in jute industry for example, which stood at 287,000 in 1921 decreased to 279,290 in 1931; in collieries from 181,000 to 173,175 and in printing press from 49000 to 39935.[3] No migration was feasible so long as there was such steep fall in the demand for labour.

In the wake of those developments, there was an inflow of return migration from Malaya and other foreign lands. There was a fall in the ratio of internal migrants as a percentage to the total population due to those various unfavourable conditions. Those conditions continued to retard migratory movement till the end of the thirties.

By the end of thirties, when economy was on the path of recovery, the Second World War started in Europe. In close succession, it spread to Asia also. The War created an altogether new situation and all the efforts were diverted for the purpose of the War. However, many of those efforts had a positive impact on migration. Hundreds of thousands of youngmen were recruited to the army and naturally there was an exodus of young men from different parts of India to enroll in the military service. Attainment of independence in 1947 added altogehter new dimensions to the migratory movement in India. Millions of people were uprooted from various parts of the country leading to the refugee problem which became a daunting task for the government to handle soon after independence. Thus, migratory movement passed through different phases of ups and downs till the attainment of independence.

Inter-Regional Variations in Outmigration

Though the intensity of out-migration was very low in the country as a whole, it was very high in certain regions of the country since the turn of the century. In some regions, the volume of net migration, being the difference between in-migrants and out-migrants, was negative. In some other regions where intensity was low, the volume of net migration was positive indicating the presence of more inmigrants than outmigrants. Table 4.2 gives the number of net migrants in different presidencies/ regions of the country since independence.

The presidencies/regions with high intensity of migration were United Province, Bihar-Orissa, Madras, Rajaputana, Hyderabad and Jammu & Kashmir. There was no fall in the intensity of migration and the volume of out-migration was higher than inmigration, indicating a negative net-migration of population throughout the peirod under reference. On the other hand, Bengal, Bombay, Mysore, Travancore-Cochin, Assam, Central Province and Punjab were those with low

Table 4.2: Migration from Different Presidencies/Regions of India

Name of the Presidency/Region	*1901*	*1911*	*1921*	*1931*
United Province	-891576	-815855	-972076	-1065566
Bihar-Orissa	-141190	-1490385	-1566900	-1203877
Bengal	—	+1335624	+1129389	+761874
Assam	+699321	+757424	+1140152	+1241029
Travancore-Cochin	+64897	+60750	+65334	+119588
Mysore	+122997	+217691	+240460	-249698
Hyderabad	-6348	-57031	-168256	-90954
Bombay	+61761	+272430	+414466	+424431
Central Province	+323314	+428600	+197382	+217384
Central India	+122724	-65491	+57694	+97901
Rajaputana	-599816	-542304	-560972	-477379
Punjab	+183520	+102487	+169824	+137030
Jammu & Kashmir	-3457	-7584	-33370	-33270
Madras	-485681	-607123	-730830	-897572

Source: Adapted from K.C.Zachariah. *A Historical Study of Internal Migration in the Indian Sub-Continent 1901-1931* (Bombay, Asia Publishing House, 1964), pp. 63-64).

intensity. The inmigrants outnumbered the outmigrants in all these states. Why certain regions became inmigrating regions while others were remaining as out-migrating areas?

As already seen in Chapter 2, Assam became an inmigrating region since the middle of nineteenth century. Hundreds of thousands of workers hailing from United Provinces and Orissa-Bihar flocked to the tea gardens in Assam. Similarly, migrants began to move to Bombay with the growth of industries around Bombay. With the growing industrial activities, Bengal was also able to attract workers from other regions. In Travancore-Cochin states and Mysore state, coffee and tea plantations were opened from the middle of the nineteenth century by the European planters. Labour requirements of these plantations were met by the inmigrants from the neighbouring Madras presidency. The same trend in inmigration appeared to have continued in all these areas during the early decades of twentieth century.

Now the question is, why certain regions like Uttar Pradesh or Bihar or Madras evinced strong outmigrating tendencies while other regions were not at all sending migrants to these regions? As already stated, these regions were the places of origin of labour under indenture system. The same tradition would have persisted in the case of internal migration also. Zachariah concurs the same with the following observation: "The long established tradition of out-migration gave the would be migrants the necessary contacts and connections in the areas of destination and therefore, was an important factor in the continuance of migration even in periods of natural decrease".[4] Another authority collaborates the same thus: "In the same way, the field labourer finds his ancestral occupation not sufficiently paying, or is moved by examples of a fellow labourer who has left the village in some public work carried by government or in the mines or coffee estates in the adjacent district where better wages are offered".[5]

Rajaputana was perhaps in exception to this general pattern. Migration from Rajaputana was also brisk, though labour migration of the type mentioned earlier was absent from Rajaputana. One of the main factors would have been the general attitude of the people of Rajaputana to migrate to other regions on account of the unsettled political conditions and inclement weather conditions. Further, they would have emulated the example of Marwaris, the business community of Rajasthan. The Marwaris of Rajasthan were the pioneers of migration in the Indian sub-continent right from the time of the Mughals. During the nienteenth cnetury, they migrated to almost all parts of India as traders, moneylenders and merchants. Thomas Timberg graphically describes the Marwari presence in various parts of India with the following words:

"In Central India, the rural areas of Bombay Province, Bihar, the Marathwada areas of Hyderabad and Assam, the Marwaris became the pre-eminent local moneylenders and merchants. They financed, especially the growth of new cash crops which the British demanded. In the Brahmaputra Valley of Assam and North Bengal they had a monopoly on the export of all crops except tea and the import of all provisions. Their settlement seems to date from the opening of these areas to outside trade from 1840 onwards".[6] There is no other community in the whole of India which set its tentacles throughout India. The members belonging to other communities of Rajaputana would have emulated the example of the Marwaris who created Rajasthani networks throughout India. Not surprisingly, the migration from Rajasthan as Zachariah enjoins, "is not confined to contiguous states but stretched even to distant state such as Assam".[7]

Most of the regular migrants belonged to the category of industrial labourers or estate workers. However, another pattern of migration termed as "farmer migration" originated from Bengal presidency during the twentieth century". Farmers and peasants from Bengal started to move and clear the fertile jungle lands of Assam from the early decades of twentieth century. By tradition, Bengalis were not inclined to migrate as coolie labourers and in the words of Davis, "the Bengalis went to Assam to farm and not to work on estates".[8] While the number of Bengali farmers went on increasing the number of estate workeres declined. By 1931, the number of persons born in Bengal who migrated to Assam swelled to the extent of 575,000.[9]

Similarly, Punjab also became another theatre of peasant migration. It was set in motion by the development of new irrigation projects. It is estimated that no less than 240,000 persons left their home districts to settle in the canal areas of Punjab during the 1921–1931 decade.[10] Most of the migrants to the canal colonies came from the same province itself.

Emergence of Kerala as an Outmigratory Region

In the previous chapter, we have seen how the immobile people of Kerala started to move to distant lands. Nevertheless, as seen in the previous section, Kerala has remained as an inmigrating region even in 1931. If so, how and when Kerala could transform as an outmigrating region?

As seen in the previous chapter, education has played a key role in transforming the Malayalees as a mobile class of people. The change in attitude in favour of material comforts inculcated by the spread of education has been the crucial factor in triggering the migratory movement from Kerala in search of better economic opportunities. Education has also been instrumental in promoting migration for an altogether different reason. The progress of education has been rapid in Kerala as a whole and Travancore in particular. During 1920s as many as five lakh children were attending the educational institutions in the princely state of Travancore. With the spread of education the number of employment seekers among the educated also began to swell. However, opportunities for employment were not expanding in proportion to the spread of education. The Unemployment Enquiry Committee appointed in Travancore in 1928, came to the conclusion, "that the number of educationally qualified persons seeking employment has been in recent years very much in excess of the demand for their services".[11] According to the Committee yearly addition in different categories of educated job-seekers in the state numbered on an average 3145 persons. On the other hand, only 1360 persons could find employment in the state leaving as many as 2140 persons as unemployed. Under such circumstances the suggestion of the Committee itself was "to explore the facilities for emigration if any that may be available outside the state".[12] Around this period industrial and commercial enterprises with scope for employment opportunities were growing in the urban centres like Bombay and

Madras. No wonder, educated young men could take advantage of those opportunities and migrate to different parts of India.

Thus the migratory movement which started during the early decades could gather momentum in course of time. More and more, people began to move to far-off places in search of better economic prospects. Table 4.3 gives the number of persons born in Travancore and Cochin but enumerated in other parts of India in 1931.

Table 4.3: Number of Migrants from Travancore and Cochin States in 1931

Sl.No.	*Migrated to*	*Migrants from Travancore*	*Migrants from Cochin*
1.	Assam	1	1
2.	Bengal	8	23
3.	Bombay	618	3205
4.	Delhi	4	17
5.	Madras	16756	14820
6.	Punjab	1	—
7.	United Province	60	—
8.	Baroda	9	14
9.	Cochin	31167	—
10.	Hyderabad	28	31
11.	Mysore	422	543
12.	Rajasthan	1	2
13.	Travancore	—	26964
14.	Other States*	90	108
	Total	49165	45728

Source: *Census of India 1931, Imperial Tables.*

Note: Other States* include Coorg,Andaman and Nicobar, Bihar and Orissa, Central Indian states, Western Indian states, and Bombay states.

As can be seen from the Table 4.3, there was a significant increase in the size of migrant population both from Travancore and Cochin. However, the overwhelming majority were to the nearby regions. Outmigrants to distant places like Bombay or Delhi were not many. Nevertheless, Travancore and Cochin states were soon to become net out-migrating regions. The Second World War created the necessary conditions for such a transformation.

The War as usual created shortages, miseries and even famine in the country. However, the War was instrumental in accelerating the migratory movement especially in the case of Kerala. One of the outcomes of the War was the large scale recruitment of youngmen to the army and other defence services. In Travancore, where eduated unemployment had sufraced from the twenties, the large scale recruitment of personnel to the army became a golden opportunity for the youngsters to seek employment. The result was a rush to the recruiting offices in search of military service. The war time shortages also induced the youngmen to seek employment in distant lands. From Travancore alone, as many as 1.57 lakh persons were enrolled in the army and civilian labour force.[13] From Cochin and Malabar also hundreds of thousands of young men enrolled in the army. Not only in the army but also in other sectors of the economy connected with War, the demand for labour rose high. The net result was the transformation of Travancore and Cochin states also as outmigratory regions. According to Zachariah, the total number of inmigrants in Travancore-Cochin was respectively 38,000 during 1931–41 and 53,000 during 1941–51. Against this, outmigrants from Travancore-Cochin totalled 43,000 for the decade 1931–41 and 143,000 for the decade 1941–1951.[14] According to another estimate, the total number of Travancore-Cochin born persons living outside the state was 1.17 lakhs by 1951.[15] Thus, Travancore-Cochin region became an outmigrating region for which the Second World War became the immediate cause.

The question is, whether Malabar was also an inmigratory region? However, no accurate data relating to the magnitude of migration from Malabar are available as Malabar formed part of the Madras presidency. Nevertheless, more number of people from Malabar would have migrated to other parts of India on account of the unequitable land tenure system which prevailed in Malabar. Under the land system, tenants were pauperized and many of them were compelled to migrate for the purpose of eking out an existence. The Report of the Tenancy Committee of Malabar 1940 aptly describes the situation thus: ".... thosuands of youngmen quit Malabar in search of employment and that menial service throughout the presidency if not the whole of India has become the monopoly of the Nairs of Malabar instead of the military service of the pre-British days".[16] In fact, the large number of estate workers found in some parts of south India, were also those from Malabar. Thus, the number of estate workers from Malabar in Coimbatore district of Madras for instance totalled 1223 and in Nilgiri district 3675 in 1931.[17]

Intensity of migration would have been higher from Malabar for other reasons. In Malabar, facilities for higher education was expanding and the educated youth were on the look out for employment in various parts outside Kerala but particularly in Madras city as it was their provincial capital. Consequently, the ranks of educated Nairs, Pattar Brahmins and Thiyyas who were employed in Madras swelled. Further, those who were in government service had to move to various parts of the presidency.

In the absence of a comprehensive picture about the magnitude of migration from different parts of Kerala one has to lay hands on other sources. Linguistic distribution of population in various parts of India forms an important source. Malayalam speaking people living outside Kerala region would be either the descendants of the migrants from Kerala or migrants themselves. There was a steady increase in the size of Malayalam speaking people in various parts of India since the turn of the century. Table 4.4 given below indicates the growth in the number of Malayalee population in various parts of India.

Table 4.4: Growth of Malayalee Population in Various Parts of India excluding Kerala since 1901

Sl. No.	*Name of the Presidency/ States*	*1901*	*1921*	*1931*	*1951*
1.	Madras Presidency excluding S.Canara district	12005	30820	67277	206809
2.	Mysore State	3121	5818	8513	38664
3.	Coorg	14039	NA	24940	32683
4.	Hyderabad	31	NA	270	5235
5.	Bombay	1208	1944	11723	39848
6.	Bengal	67	NA	305	1955
7.	Bihar-Orissa	—	NA	403	241
8.	United Provinces	13	NA	396	2001
9.	Central Provinces	12	NA	349	2365
10.	Baroda	—	—	112	NA
11.	Rajaputana (Ajmer)	—	—	5	—
12.	Birar	11	—	—	—
13.	Punjab	5	—	27	112
14.	Delhi	—	—	—	9805
15.	Andamans	—	—	2073	2813
16.	Assam	—	—	62	234
17.	Others	48	—	539	333
	Total	30560	—	116994	343098

Source: *Census of India Linguistic Tables*, Various years.

As the Table indicates there was significant increase in the size of Malayalam speaking population in various parts of India since the turn of the century. In 1901 when migration was in the offing, there were only 30560 Malayalees in areas outside the present Kerala. Most of them were in Coorg (14039), Coimbatore (1350), Nilgiris (4759), Madurai (1862), Tinnevelly (1065); all adjacent areas of Kerala.[18] The number of Malayalee population increased to 116,994 by 1931, an increase of more than three times. The number went upto 343,098 in 1951, an increase of more than ten times since 1901. Evidently, much of the increase has taken place between 1931 and 1951.

Among the various states, Madras topped the list for accounting more than two thirds of the Malayalam speaking population in areas outside Kerala. A number of reasons can be attributed to the presence of overwhelming number of Malayalees in Madras presidency. Being a district of the then Madras presidency, people from Malabar had to go to Madras and other parts of the presidency for various administrative purposes. The need for higher education and medical treatment were equally important reasons which attracted Malayalees in large numbers to Madras city proper. Since Madras was growing as the most important industrial and business centre in the south, large numbers of Malayalees both educated and uneducated were attracted to Madras. While the majority of the educated class were absorbed in white collar occupations, the less educated were absorbed in various unskilled occupations. Some of them even started their own petty business enterprises. An author gives the following graphic description about the activities of the less affluent Malayalee migrants in Madras city thus:

"The poor class of Hindus, Muslims and Christians as they began to settle in the city since the Second World War established a number of retail stores in Madras, and Malayalees can now be found throughout the city employed in tea stalls, beedi stalls, egg or vegetable marts, hair-dressing saloons, book-stalls, textile shops, bakeries, hotels or driving auto-rickshaws or taxis. They are also employed as unskilled factory workers, and as machinists, welders and mechanics. Many who entered the city penniless in the 1940s now own their own small shops and stalls, and although they may not earn more than Rupees 400 a month, they are economically independent".[19] Though overwhelming majority among them were from Malabar, those from Travancore and Cochin were also fairly in large numbers.

The former princely state of Mysore accounted for more than 10 per cent of emigrant Malayalee population. If we add with this the number of persons in Coorg, then a centrally administered state, which was subsequently merged with Mysore in 1956, the total Malayalee population in Mysore would be more than 20 per cent. Mysore could attract increasing number of Malayalees apparently due to its proximity to Kerala. Malayalee migrants were found in a wide variety occupations. The census report of the former Mysore state for the year 1951 aptly describes the callings of the Malayalees in Mysore thus:

"They combine the hardihood of the Tulu worker, the enterprise of the Konganies and they are far more catholic in the choice of occupations than either. They discover opportunities everywhere and seize them by the forelock wherever they are found. Many of them engage in the clerical, supervisory and technical categories of occupations. Some among them were pedlars, hawkers and factory hands".[20] There were also lawyers, doctors, engineers and senior civil servants among them. Estate workers constituted a significant section of the Malayalee migrants in Coorg.

The share of Bombay, a far away presidency from Kerala was more than 10 per cent of the total Malayalee migrants in 1951. Most of them were white collar workers of various categories. The presence of Malayalee white collar workers became conspicuous from the time of the Second World War when the central government opened Control Offices of the War and started to recruit large number of white collar employees.[21] Fairly large number of Malayalees were found in industrial and commercial enterprises as technical and non-technical hands. In other provinces/states like Bengal, Hyderabad, Central Provinces, Delhi etc. sizeable number of Malayalees could be found. Most of the Malayalees in Delhi were employed in various departments of the central government. In brief, the presence of Malayalees could be found in almost all parts of India and they became a widely distributed linguistic community in India by the middle of twentieth century.

Peasant Migration from Travancore to Malabar

One significant pattern of migration which emerged during the pre-independence period was the peasant migration from Travancore region to the then Malabar district. This pattern was unique in nature for a variety of reasons. Unlike the various patterns of migration from the rest of India, peasant migration from Travancore exhibited certain distinguishing characteristics. Firstly, migration, especially during the initial stages was by and large an assisted labour migration in which the migrants received assistance and encouragement from various sources including the state. On the other hand, the peasant migration was purely a voluntary one in nature in which the migrants moved by their own free volition.

Secondly, peasant migration had few parallels in India. Migration of peasants for the purpose of reclamation of wasteland was unheard of till the end of nineteenth century. The only parallel to the peasant migration was the migration of Bengali peasants to Assam. As seen earlier, large number of Bengali peasants had migrated and settled down in various parts of Brahmaputra Valley in Assam by the thirties. Similarly, streams of peasants from Travancore migrated and settled down in the sub-mountaineous regions of the erstwhile Malabar district.

Thirdly, with the possible exception of a few professional and trader migrants, overwhelming majority of the migrants from the rest of India were poor people with practically no resource worth the name. They were so poor that they migrated for the sake of survival. It was by and large, a coolie affair which, as already stated brought discredit to the country. On the other hand, the peasant migrants from Travancore possessed bits of capital of their own which they utilised for furthering their own economic prospects.

Lastly, the overwhelming majority of the migrants from the rest of India belonged to the lowest strata of society. In sharp contrast to this, the peasant migrants enjoyed respectable place in the social hierarchy of Kerala.[22] Majority of them belonged to the Syrian Christian community from the northern half of Travancore.

According to the 1951 census, the total number of persons who migrated from Travancore to Malabar region was 88275. Of them, 78148 persons were to the rural tracts of Malabar district.[23] Most of them were peasant farmers from Travancore who occupied the uncultivated barren lands in the interior parts of the Malabar district. Inter-state migration of similar nature also took place to Coorg, then a centrally administered state and to South Canara district of the former Madras presidency on a limited scale.[24]

New Dimensions in the Patterns of Migration during the Post-Independence Period

There was a lull in all patterns of migration during the years following the Second World War and partition of the country. It could be attributed to a number of factors. Over utilization of the machinery and equipment during the War period had rendered the whole industrial set up in a run down condition. There was acute shortage of food and consumer goods in the country. Added to these, the partition of the country had caused on abrupt division of the economy into two or rather three parts. Partition created dislocation and confusion everywhere. The forced migration of millions of people as an aftermath of partition created further difficulties. Unemployment became acute on account of these developments and also on account of the retrenchment of large number of military personnel recruited during the War period. Needless to say, all these factors contributed to the decline in the flow of internal migration of the people.

However, the massive developmental programmes initiated soon after independence were potential factors conducive to rejuvenate migratory movement within the country. The gigantic industrial ventures like the Fertilizer Corporations, Steel Complexes, Heavy Machine Factories etc. established in various parts of the country required the services of a large number of workers of different trade. They could serve as pull factors to the migratory movement of people from those regions like Kerala which had a lead in educational development.

The State Reorganization of 1956, on linguistic basis was another development which could affect migratory movement both positively and negatively. As an immediate effect, the people of the then Part B and C states could move freely with a sense of equality to all parts of India. One of the favourable impacts of the State Reorganization was the possibility for obtaining comprehensive data on migration from states like Andhra Pradesh, Karnataka, Kerala etc. For Kerala, it was an event which integrated the three divisions of Malayalam speaking areas into one political unit. However, the Reorganization of the states on linguistic basis as such was a development which could adversely affect migration in the years to come.

As a result of these developments, migratory movement which received a setback immediately after the attainment of independence began to revive in full swing. New dimensions were added to the whole process. More and more people began to move in search of better economic opportunities thrown open with the opening of the industrial complexes. Table 4.5 gives the overall picture of interstate migration in India as on 1961.

As can be seen from the Table, there was marked increase in the volume of internal migration by 1960s. During the early decades of twentieth century, the intensity of migration reckoned in terms of the volume of migration as a percentage to the total population was around 2.5 or even less. It has gone upto 3.33 by 1961. The actual volume of the migrants increased from 8.9 millions in 1931 to well over 14 millions in 1961. It works out to an increase of more than 75 per cent.

As in the past, the intensity of inmigration was very high in states like Maharashtra, West Bengal, Madhya Pradesh, Karnataka and Assam. On the other hand, intensity of outmigration was very high in states like Punjab, Rajasthan, Uttar Pradesh, Bihar, Orissa, Kerala, Gujarat, Jammu and Kashmir etc. Among them, Kerala and Punjab were inmigrating regions in the past. As already stated, the transition of Kerala as an outmigrating region took place during the Second World War period. Since then, outmigration was very brisk and Kerala could overtake Tamil Nadu, Andhra Pradesh, Orissa etc. in intensity of outmigration. In the case of Punjab, the situation is slightly confusing. The data relating to the pre-independence period of Punjab are not comparable

Table 4.5: Intensity of Migration in Various States in 1961

Sl. No.	*Name of the State*	*Total number of inmigrants*	*Total number of out-migrants*	*Outmigrants as a percentage of state population*	*Out-migrants as a % to total migrants*
1.	Andhra Pradesh	584,021	870,294	2.41	5.94
2.	Assam	489,928	116,112	0.97	0.79
3.	Bihar	840,956	2,042,680	4.39	13.95
4.	Gujarat	528,565	734,692	3.56	5.01
5.	Jammu and Kashmir	31,948	78,764	2.21	0.53
6.	Karnataka (Mysore)	1,040,331	794,110	3.36	5.42
7.	Kerala	233,416	624,444	3.69	4.26
8.	Madhya Pradesh	1,479,312	824,960	2.54	5.63
9.	Maharashtra	2,550,278	867,687	2.19	5.92
10.	Orissa	332,078	471,891	2.68	3.22
11.	Punjab	712,039	1,318,840	6.49	9.0
12.	Rajasthan	646,382	1,112,361	5.51	7.59
13.	Tamil Nadu (Madras)	587,745	1,095,590	3.25	7.48
14.	Uttar Pradesh	1,105,961	2,583,879	3.5	17.64
15.	West Bengal	2,239,354	605,903	1.74	4.13
16.	Delhi	971,725	183,356	6.89	1.25
17.	Himachal Pradesh	71,618	67,830	5.02	0.46
18.	Others	195,279	247,543	—	1.69
	All India	14,640,936	14,640,936	3.33	100.00

Source: *Census of India 1961, Vol. I, Part II C(IV), Migration Tables.*

with those of the post-independence period as the data of pre-independence period included those areas transferred to Pakistan. Further, brisk migration was taking place from Punjab to various parts of India and to foreign lands, though in migration was also fairly on a large scale. Moreover, Punjab as seen earlier was a state experiencing peasant migration in the past.[25] Nevertheless, the emergence of Punjab as the top-ranking state in intensity of outmigration is a significant development of the post-independence period. The actual volume of migration was the highest in Uttar Pradesh followed by Bihar. Pre-independence pattern appears to have held good in the case of both the states. Though Tamil Nadu and Andhra Pradesh continued to be outmigrating states, the intensity of outmigration has declined considerably in both the states. With an intensity of outmigration well over the all India level, changes on a significant scale have taken place in the case of Kerala. Only Punjab, Bihar and Rajasthan were ahead of Kerala in intensity of outmigration in 1961.

Notwithstanding the belated emergence of Kerala as an outmigrating state, migrants can be found in almost all parts of India as Tables 4.6

and 4.7 indicate. However, as can be seen from the Tables, the overwhelming majority of the migrants congregated in three states; viz., Madras (Tamil Nadu), Mysore (Karnataka) and Maharashtra. With the presence of 44 per cent of the migrants from Kerala, Tamil Nadu continued to remain as the destination of the largest congregation of Keralites. Though the percentage of Malayalee population in Tamil Nadu has gone down from 70 per cent in 1931 to 44 per cent in 1961, the actual number of migrant population in Tamil Nadu has gone up to 276,518 in 1961 on the basis of birth place returns. Reckoned in terms of mother tongue, the other yardstick to estimate the magnitude of the migrant population, the Malayalee population in Tamil Nadu totalled 4 lakh and odd in 1961. The number of the migrants on the basis of language was much larger than on the basis of birth-place returns. Since the Malayalee migration to the Madras presidency goes back to the closing decades of nineteenth century, many of the Malayalees in Madras would be the descendants of the earlier migrants who do not figure in the birth place returns. Signifiantly, by 1961, migrants from Kerala to Madras outnumbered the migrants from Madras to Kerala. Thus a reversal in the relative role of the two states in the intensity of in and out migration has taken place. Though the push-pull combination

Table 4.6: Size of Migrants from Kerala in Different Parts of India as on 1961

Sl. No.	*Name of the State*	*Number of Persons*	*Males*	*Females*
1.	Andhra Pradesh	24,898 (3.98)	17,513	7,385
2.	Assam	2,182 (0.34)	1,807	375
3.	Bihar	7,135 (1.14)	4,170	2,965
4.	Gujarat	7,849 (1.25)	5,812	2,037
5.	Jammu and Kashmir	194 (0.03)	145	49
6.	Karnataka (Mysore)	137,220 (21.97)	90,779	46,441
7.	Madhya Pradesh	18248 (2.92)	14,386	3,862
8.	Maharashtra	98,094 (15.70)	71,325	26,769
9.	Orissa	4,262 (0.68)	3,641	621
10.	Punjab	5,648 (0.90)	4,618	1,030
11.	Rajasthan	1,997 (0.31)	1,318	649
12.	Tamil Nadu (Madras)	276,518 (44.28)	162,331	114,187
13.	Uttar Pradesh	5,673 (0.90)	4,328	1,345
14.	West Bengal	12,419 (1.98)	9,063	3,356
15.	Delhi	10,232 (1.63)	6,480	3,752
16.	Andaman & Nicobar	3,735 (0.59)	2,574	1,161
17.	Others	8,140 (1.3)	4,955	3,185
	Total	624,444 (100)	405,275	219,169

Note: Figures in the bracket indicate per cent.
Source: *Census of India 1961*, Vol.I, Part II-C (IV), *Migration Tables*.

Table 4.7: Distribution of Malayalee Population in Various Parts of India as on 1961

Sl. No.	*Name of the State*	*Size of Malayalee Population*	*Males*	*Females*
1.	Andhra Pradesh	23,350 (2.56)	16,225	7,125
2.	Assam	2,204 (0.23)	1,915	289
3.	Bihar	7,559 (1.23)	4,602	2,957
4.	Gujarat	7,785 (0.85)	5,767	2,018
5.	Jammu and Kashmir	156 (0.03	110	46
6.	Karnataka (Mysore)	305,512 (33.55)	176,566	128,946
7.	Madhya Pradesh	19924 (2.22)	15,333	4,591
8.	Maharashtra	90,460 (9.94)	65,603	24,857
9.	Orissa	4,832 (0.52)	3,436	1,396
10.	Punjab	6,395 (0.70)	5,178	1,217
11.	Rajasthan	2,213 (0.24)	1,240	973
12.	Tamil Nadu (Madras)	404,346 (44.46)	229,541	174,805
13.	Uttar Pradesh	7,715 (0.85)	5,299	2,416
14.	West Bengal	8,602 (0.94)	6,489	2,113
15.	Delhi	9489(1.04)	5961	3528
16.	Andaman & Nicobar	6673(0.73)	4015	2658
17.	Others	2105 (0.21)	1,953	521
	Total	909,320 (100)	549233	360,087

Source: *Census of India 1961 Language Tables*, Table C(V), A Distribution of Mother Tongue.

Notes: 1. Figures do not include the Malayalee population of Kerala, Pondicherry and Lakshadweep.

2. Figures in the bracket indicate percentage to the total.

was not very favourable for large scale migration, more and more Malayalees could come and settle down in Madras on account of the historical connections that existed between Kerala and Tamil Nadu and also on account of the proximity of the two states.

Migrants to the former Mysore State (Karnataka) totalled 137,220 on the basis of birth place returns. On the other hand, the number of Malayalees in the state totalled 305,512 in 1961. How could so many Malayalees be found in Karnataka when the actual number of migrants does not come even half the size of Malayalee population? One of the important reasons for the presence of such a large number of Malayalees in the state was the merger of the former Coorg state, where a considerable number of Malayalees resided in the past, with the Mysore state at the time of State Reorganisation in 1956. Similarly, South Canara district which had a sizable Malayalee population was also added to the Mysore state in 1956. Furthermore, migration of peasants from Travancore had also taken place in the districts like South Canara and

Coorg of Mysore state at the time of peasant migration from Travancore to Malabar.[26] All these factors could account for the presence of a much larger number of Malayalees in Mysore, than the actual number of migrants.

With 98,000, inmigrants from Kerala, the share of Bombay (Maharashtra) has gone upto 15 per cent of the total number of migrants from Kerala. On the other hand, in 1901, there were hardly 1000 persons speaking Malayalam as their mother tongue in the then Bombay presidency. It has gone upto 90,460 by 1961. The increase was more than 90 times the size of the Malayalee population of 1901. The pull factors could be more powerful in the case of Bombay; a far away state from Kerala, than any other factor to the large scale migration from Kerala. Interestingly, the number of Malayalee population in Bombay was much lower than that of the number of migrants in 1961. Apparently, it could be due to the absence of any large scale settlement of Malayalees in Bombay. Another important reason would be the presence of non-Malayalam speaking population among the migrants from Kerala. Non-Malayalee elements like the Pattar Brahmin and Konkani Brahmin settlers of Kerala have also been migrating in large numbers from Kerala.

Nearly 82 per cent of the migrants from Kerala was concentrated in these three states. However, the ranks of the migrants from Kerala to states like Andhra Pradesh, Madhya Pradesh, West Bengal, Delhi etc. have also been swelling. In Delhi for example, Malayalam speaking population was nil in 1931. Their number has gone well over 9,000 by 1961. Thus Keralites have become a fully mobile class of people by 1961. As mentioend earlier, the number of Malayalam speaking people in areas located outside the present Kerala state was only 30560 in 1901. It went upto 343,098 in 1951. By 1961, it has gone upto 9 lakhs. They formed nearly 5.34 per cent of the total Malayalee population in the whole of India.

Later Trends in the Pattern of Migration

The momentum gained in the migratory movement during the fifties could continue for various reasons. More and more factories requiring the services of large number of workers were opened in the country during the sixties and the seventies. Furthermore, the development in transport and communications could facilitate the quick movement of people from region to region. How far the intensity of migration was affected in various parts of the country in the wake of these development would be explored in the section that follow.

The Census Reports of 1971 and 1981 contain data on various aspects of internal migration in India. Tables 4.8 and 4.9 based on census data of 1971 and 1981 indicate the intensity of migration in different states in India in 1971 and 1981 respectively.

As can be seen, West Bengal accommodated more number of inmigrants from various parts of India than any other state. Maharashtra came second. As in the past, the other states which received more number of inmigrants were Madhya Pradesh, Assam, Haryana, Punjab, Karnataka, Gujarat and Delhi. Delhi, the capital of India was attracting streams of migrants from the beginning of the century.

Among the outmigrating states, intensity was the highest in the case of Punjab followed by Haryana in 1971. Interestingly, intensity of inmigration was also pretty high in the cases of Punjab and Haryana. In fact, Punjab and Haryana were two states with high intensity in inmigration and outmigration even earlier. Haryana recorded the highest rate of intensity followed by Punjab. The other states with high intensity in the descending order were Delhi, Himachal Pradesh, Rajasthan and Kerala. Intensity of outmigration has declined from 5.3 per cent in the case of Rajasthan in 1971 to 4.96 per cent in 1981. On the other hand, the intensity of outmigration improved from 4.41 in 1971 to 4.44 per cent in the case of Kerala. While the intensity of outmigration increased from 3.91 per cent in 1971 to 4.41 per cent in 1981 in Uttar Pradesh, it declined from 3.90 per cent to 3.59 per ent in Bihar. In all other states intensity of outmigration was lower than the national average. Among the various states in India, the intensity of migration has recorded any improvement only in the case of Punjab, Haryana and Kerala. Though there was a decrease in intensity of migration in the case of Uttar Pradesh and Bihar, the volume of outmigration continued to remain large in the case of both Uttar Pradesh and Bihar.

While the migratory movement was steadily maintaining the momentum, certain developments capable of retarding it were in the offing. One of them was the Khalistan movement in Punjab which took an ugly turn leading to the "Operation blue star" in 1982. Though it did not affect the outmigration of the Punjabis, inmigration to Punjab was adversely affected. In Assam, the agitation against the foreign nationals also took a violent turn. With the agitation gaining momentum, Assamese began to look upon inmigrant groups from other parts of India with suspicion and even with hostility. Linguistic cum ethnic disturbances of lesser magnitude took place in Tamil Nadu and Maharashtra. Anti-Malayalee agitations took place in certain parts of Tamil Nadu. Similarly, south Indians were the targets of attack by the activists of Shiv Sena in

Table 4.8 : Intensity of Migration in Various States in 1971

Sl. No.	*Name of the State*	*No. of inmigrants*	*No. of outmigrants*	*Percentage of migrants as ratio to the state population*	*Percentage of out-migrants to the total number of migrants*
1.	Andhra Pradesh	746158	1061278	2.43	6.59
2.	Assam	1522461	192876	1.31	1.03
3.	Bihar	1176408	2201399	3.90	11.82
4.	Gujarat	944264	865187	3.24	4.64
5.	Haryana	1406780	837519	8.34	4.49
6.	Himachal Pradesh	180431	223268	6.45	1.19
7.	Jammu & Kashmir	111254	80865	1.75	0.43
8.	Karnataka	1187768	1120698	3.82	6.01
9.	Kerala	270665	942639	4.41	5.06
10.	Madhya Pradesh	2106691	977153	2.34	5.24
11.	Maharashtra	3625192	1139809	2.26	6.12
12.	Orissa	586787	493501	2.24	2.64
13.	Punjab	1666536	1193277	8.80	6.40
14.	Rajasthan	1118202	1366082	5.30	7.33
15.	Tamil Nadu	969302	1083434	2.62	5.81
16.	Uttar Pradesh	1748638	3460923	3.91	18.58
17.	West Bengal	5331517	779982	1.76	4.18
18.	Delhi	1960822	280354	6.89	1.50
19.	Others		323272		1.73
	Total	18623514	18623514	3.39	100.00

Source: *Census of India Geographic Distribution of Internal Migration 1971-1981* (New Delhi, 1989).

Table 4.9 : Intensity of Migration in Various States as on 1981

Sl. No.	Name of the State	Total No. of inmigrants	Total No. of outmigrants	Outmigrants as a percentage to state population	Outmigrants as a percentage to total migrants
1.	Andhra Pradesh	899947	1337578	2.49	5.56
2.	Assam	—	292481	N.A.	1.21
3.	Bihar	1330919	2512430	3.59	10.45
4.	Gujarat	1299043	1061505	3.11	4.41
5.	Haryana	1625607	1155474	8.94	4.81
6.	Himachal Pradesh	231255	280139	6.54	1.16
7.	Jammu & Kashmir	123052	97066	1.62	0.40
8.	Karnataka	1664941	1503344	4.04	6.25
9.	Kerala	360435	1131598	4.44	4.71
10.	Madhya Pradesh	2361680	1494378	2.86	6.22
11.	Maharashtra	4677529	1499705	2.38	6.24
12.	Orissa	761772	537807	2.03	2.23
13.	Punjab	1740037	1311398	7.81	5.45
14.	Rajasthan	1471513	1699931	4.96	7.07
15.	Tamil Nadu	1207841	1447193	2.98	6.02
16.	Uttar Pradesh	1956614	4898833	4.41	20.39
17.	West Bengal	5584305	963489	1.76	4.01
18.	Delhi	2820720	407731	6.55	1.69
19.	Others		388324	—	1.61
	Total		24020404	3.50	100.00

Source: *Census of India Geographic Distribution of Internal Migration 1971-1981* (New Delhi, 1989).

Mumbai. All these ugly developments reflecting the growing nativist sentiment could adversely affect migratory movement in the country. The question is to what extent migratory movement has been retarded?

The impacts of these developments on migration are well reflected in the census report of 1991 dealing with migration. Table 4.10 gives the magnitude and intensity of migration from various states in 1991.

As can be seen from the Table the increase in the volume of migration was only marginal to that of 1981. The actual volume was only 27.29 millions as against 24 millions in 1981. The intensity of migration has been 3.22 per cent in 1991 as against 3.50 per cent in 1981. Needless to say some sort of deceleration in the migratory movement has set in. Apparently, the decade 1971-1981 was the peak period in the migratory movement in India. The reasons as stated earlier could be the emergence of nativist movements in regions like Assam, Maharashtra, Tamil Nadu, Karnataka etc. which looked upon ethnic groups migrated from other regions with suspicion and even with hostility.

Among the states in India, intensity of migration was the highest in Haryana, the percentage being 8.59 followed by Punjab. Delhi, Rajasthan and Uttar Pradesh occupying respectively the second, third and fourth ranks in the gradation of intensity of migration. With a percentage of 3.85 Kerala's ranking has gone down below to that of Uttar Pradesh and Bihar. Even in the volume of migration, there was a fall in the actual number of migrants from 11.35 lakhs in 1981 to 11.23 lakhs in 1991. As a percentage to the all India total, the volume of outmigration from Kerala was 5.06 in 1971. It has declined to 4.71 in 1981 and to 4.11 in 1991. Evidently, a declining trend has set in, since the seventies. In this connection, the findings of another study point to the emergence of a new trend in the pattern of migration from Kerala. In the words of the authors of the study: "There are two distinct phases (or turn around) in the historical trend in the migration experience of Kerala. The first turn around occurred in the 1940s when Kerala became closely integrated in the other states in India. It started with World War II, and the Indian Independence in 1947. Until then, Kerala was a net-in-migration state; more persons from neighbouring states came to Kerala than the number of persons who moved to these states. After the integration for the first time, Kerala became a net out migration state. The number of persons from Kerala moving to Madras, Bombay, Calcutta, Delhi and other metropolitan centres exceeded the number who came to Kerala from other states".

"The second turn around took place in 1970s, when Kerala became

Table 4.10: Intensity of Migration in Various States as on 1991

Sl. No.	*Name of the State*	*Total No.of immigrants*	*Total No. of outmigrants*	*Outmigrants as a percentage to state population*	*Outmigrants as a percentage to total Outmigrants*
1.	Andhra Padesh	1026863	1292774	1.94	4.73
2.	Assam	536579	347149	1.54	1.27
3.	Bihar	1049969	3147295	3.64	11.52
4.	Gujarat	1520421	927231	2.24	3.39
5.	Haryana	1550569	1415574	8.59	5.18
6.	Himachal Pradesh	224911	353156	3.07	1.29
7.	Jammu and Kashmir	N.A.	131817	1.71	0.48
8.	Karnataka	1653344	1497029	3.32	5.48
9.	Kerala	398470	1123006	3.85	4.11
10	Madhya Pradesh	2596005	1488632	2.24	5.45
11	Maharashtra	4211530	1737421	2.20	6.36
12	Orissa	592292	635089	2.00	2.32
13	Punjab	1126149	1373356	6.76	5.03
14	Rajasthan	1466134	1999090	4.54	7.32
15	Tamil Nadu	890127	1529102	2.55	5.60
16	Uttar Pradesh	1870226	5975284	4.29	21.88
17	West Bengal	2024165	1141680	1.67	4.18
18	Delhi	3333161	489774	5.17	1.79
19	Others	1229028	695486	3.22	1.81
20	Total	272,99,945	272,99,945		

Source: *Census of India 1991: Migration Tables, Part V D, Series, Vol.I, India.*

a major emigration state. Until then, international migration from Kerala was relatively small, at least compared to internal migration. The relative position of emigrants and out-migrants changed drastically after the oil-boom of the 1970s. In the 1981-91 decade, net external migration (net emigration) was about 555 thousand persons compared with net internal migration (net out migration) of 189 thousand persons".[27] Thus there was a definite fall in the net volume of outmigration. However, the fall was compensated by the external migration.

Distribution of Migrants from Kerala in Various States

Notwithstanding the declining trend, the migrants from Kerala have spread out in all parts of India. Tables 4.11 and 4.12 provide the distribution of Malayalee migrants in various parts of India.

Table 4.11 : Magnitude of Migration from Kerala in 1971

Sl. No.	*Name of the State*	*No of Migrants*	*% to total*	*No of Malayalees*	*% to total*
1.	Andhra Pradesh	36296	3.85	39913	2.87
2.	Assam	4620	0.49	5521	0.39
3.	Bihar	11010	1.16	13831	0.99
4.	Gujarat	18090	1.91	18677	0.37
5.	Haryana	1795	0.19	1647	0.11
6.	Himachal Pradesh	1349	0.14	1425	0.10
7.	Jammu & Kashmir	1465	0.15	1564	0.11
8.	Madhya Pradesh	38927	4.12	46465	3.34
9.	Maharashtra	171171	18.15	181858	13.08
10.	Karnataka (Mysore)	180766	19.17	425196	30.59
11.	Orissa	8451	0.59	11468	0.82
12.	Punjab	1971	0.20	2019	0.14
13.	Rajasthan	8015	0.85	8395	0.60
14.	Tamil Nadu	381353	40.45	559186	40.23
15.	Uttar Pradesh	16254	1.72	11035	0.79
16.	West Bengal	13706	1.45	14155	1.01
17.	Andaman & Nicobar	7289	0.77	13453	1.00
18.	Delhi	19386	2.05	19781	1.42
19.	Others	20725	2.19	13588	0.97
20.	Total	942639	100.00	1389677	100.00

Source:Census of India Geographical Distribution of Internal Migration 1971-1981 (New Delhi, 1989).

The Tables indicate that the volume of migration has gone up from 942,639 in 1971 to 1,131,598 in 1981. The volume of Malayalam speaking population outside Kerala was 1,289,000 in 1971. It formed

Table 4.12 : Magnitude of Migration from Kerala to Various States Over the Years 1981

Sl. No.	*Name of the State*	*No of Migrants*	*% to the total*	*No of Malayalees*	*% to the total*
1.	Andhra Pradesh	41966	3.70	44489	2.68
2.	Assam	N.A.	N.A.	N.A.	N.A.
3.	Bihar	12585	1.12	13760	0.83
4.	Gujarat	32145	2.84	30610	1.84
5.	Haryana	4258	0.37	4423	0.26
6.	Himachal Pradesh	1034	0.09	1034	0.06
7.	Jammu & Kashmir	1278	0.11	1135	0.06
8.	Karnataka	240199	21.22	590709	35.64
9.	Madhya Pradesh	50856	4.49	59928	3.61
10.	Maharashtra	215937	19.08	220871	13.32
11.	Orissa	10334	0.91	13586	0.81
12.	Punjab	2402	0.21	3591	0.21
13.	Rajasthan	20483	1.81	12679	0.76
14.	Tamil Nadu	409312	36.17	577890	34.87
15.	Uttar Pradesh	12789	1.13	5410	0.32
16.	West Bengal	11333	1.00	10478	0.63
17.	Andaman & Nicobar	9201	0.81	18662	1.12
18.	Delhi	31636	2.79	31143	1.87
19.	Others	23850	2.10	16777	1.01
20.	Total	1131598	100.00	1657125	100.00

Source: *Census of India Geographical Distribution of Internal Migration 1971-1981* (New Delhi, 1989).

6.33 percentage to the total Malayalees in India. The number of Malayalees outside Kerala has gone upto 1657128 by 1981.

Changes have taken place in the distribution of migrants from Kerala among various states in India. Madras continued to be the destination of the largest number of migrants. However, the percentage has declined from 40 in 1971 to 36.17 in 1981. Karnataka continued to be the destination of the second largest contingent of migrants from Kerala. The percentage has gone up from 19 in 1971 to 22 in 1981. One interesting aspect relates to the change in the percentage of Malayalees outside Kerala. By 1981, Karnataka could surpass Tamil Nadu in accommodating more number of Malayalees. There were 5.9 lakh Malayalees in Karnataka against 5.77 in Tamil Nadu. This could be due to the preference of Malayalees to settle down in Karnataka instead of Tamil Nadu, apparently on account of the anti-Malayalee sentiment prevailing in Tamil Nadu during the seventies.

Maharashtra held the third position in so far as the volume of migration from Kerala is concerned. There were 171,171 migrants in Maharashtra from Kerala in 1971. It increased to 215,537 in 1981. In terms of percentage, the migrants in Maharashtra formed 18.15 in 1971 and 19.08 in 1981. However, Malayalee population in Maharashtra formed 13 per cent of the total persons outside Kerala. The proportion of second generation of Malayalees might be low in Maharashtra.

These three states accounted for 77 per cent of the migrants in 1971. With only 76 per cent in 1981 in these three states, there was not much change in 1981. The percentage of Malayalee population in these three states was slightly higher. They formed 83.83 per cent of the total Malayalees outside Kerala in 1981. Gujarat and Delhi are two states where the number of migrants from Kerala/(Malayalees) has recorded an increase. It increased respectively from 1.99 per cent in 1971 to 2.84 per cent in Gujarat and from 2.05 per cent to 2.79 per cent in Delhi. On the other hand, there was a decline in the percentage in West Bengal.

Latest Developments in the Migratory Movement

As already stated, there was a decelerating trend in the outflow of Keralites to other parts of India from 1980s. This trend, set in motion during1980s seems to have held since then. It is well reflected in the census data of 1991. On the other hand, there was a definite increase in the magnitude of Malayalee population distributed in various states outside Kerala. (See Table 4.13).

Apparently, many Malayalees would have opted to settle down in other parts of India though the magnitude of outmigration has been on the path of decline. The actual size of Malayalees living outside Kerala was two-times the size of outmigrants from Kerala in 1991. This could be due to the growth of the Malayalee population through birth among the migrants over the years. Most of them would be the offspring of the earlier migrants.

As has been the case in 1981, Karnataka contains the largest number of Malayalees living in any state outside Kerala. However, the largest number of migrants from Kerala has been in Tamil Nadu as in the past. Apparently, migrants from Kerala prefer Karnataka to Tamil Nadu as a better place for the purpose of settlement. Maharashtra continues to be an attractive destination of large number of migrants as well as settlers from Kerala. These three states accounted for about 80 per cent of the Malayalees living in other parts of India. However, in 1981 these three states accounted for 83 per cent of the Malayalees living in the states other than Kerala. Evidently increasing numbers of Malayalees seem to

Table 4.13: Distribution of Outmigrants from Kerala and the Malayalee Population in Various Parts of India in 1991

Sl. No.	*Name of the State*	*Outmigrants*	*Malayalee Population*		
			Total	*Males*	*Females*
1.	Andhra Pradesh	50851	66409	37228	29181
2.	Assam	3378	3575	2136	1439
3.	Bihar	9840	15157	7630	7527
4	Gujarat	45220	57701	33862	23839
5.	Jammu and Kashmir	N.A.	NA	NA	NA
6.	Haryana	7670	8038	4312	3726
7.	Himachal Pradesh	1235	1257	812	445
8.	Karnataka	229557	757030	397802	359228
9.	Madhya Pradesh	69204	80759	44185	36574
10.	Maharashtra	198490	340597	199829	140768
11.	Orissa	10090	16246	9396	6850
12.	Punjab	5850	7139	4324	2815
13.	Rajasthan	18410	26450	14540	11910
14.	Tamil Nadu	356287	661137	343671	317466
15.	Uttar Pradesh	18812	15721	9110	6611
16.	West Bengal	9710	17215	9579	7636
17.	Andaman and Nicobar	9751	26075	14152	11923
18.	Delhi	45123	64952	35207	29745
19.	Goa	8501	12962	8113	4849
20.	Others	25027	20310	14611	5699
	Total	1123006	2198730*	1190499	1008231

Source: *Census of India 1991*
(i) *Migration Tables*; (ii) *Language Tables*.
Note: * Excludes the Malayalee Population of Kerala, Lakshadweep and Pondicherry.

settle in many other parts of India. Delhi, Madhya Pradesh, Gujarat, Andhra Pradesh and so on are some of the other states in which more and more Malayalees opt to settle down as years go.

One of the recent developments is the inflow of inmigrants on an increasing scale from other states. As already stated Kerala has transformed itself as an outmigrating state during the forties of the last century. At the same time inmigration has been on the decline. The total magnitude of inmigration consisted of 2.4 lakh persons in 1961.[28] However, the quantum of inmigration started to increase since 1970s. The number of inmigrants swelled to 4.37 lakh persons by 1991. With as many as 272951 inmigrants, Tamil Nadu topped the list in sending the largest contingent to Kerala in 1991 followed by Karnataka, Maharashtra, Andhra Pradesh etc. Inmigrants also hail from almost all the regions including the far away states like Jammu and Kashmir, Assam, Punjab etc.[29]

An impression is created that the large scale inmigration into Kerala is primarily due to the exodus of Keralites to foreign lands and to other parts of India. The vacuum created in the labour market on account of the outflow of large number of people is believed to be filled by the influx of workers from outside the state. Their services are being utilized on an increasing scale in the construction sector and various agricultural activities where labour shortages are being experienced.

The induction of hundreds of thousands of labourers from outside the state amounts to an anomalous development during a period when Kerala itself faces large scale unemployment. How hundreds of thousands of inmigrants can be employed in the state when the number of job seekers in the state according to the live registers of the employment exchanges has been swelling every year is the problem.[30] The situation may perhaps be related to the socio-cultural heritage of Kerala. By and large, Kerala has no tradition for hard-work and the general attitude in the society has been to look down upon manual labour. With the spread of education the educated youth started to abandom agriculture and other traditional callings. The Unemployment Enquiry Committee appointed in Travancore observed as far back as 1928 that "the fall in the actual workers engaged in agriculture can be explained by the fact that the people are abandoning agriculture for more attractive occupations".[31] As a matter of fact, many of them have been even prepared to remain idle instead of getting employed in agricultural activities. Though the agricultural wage rates were rising significantly as an aftermath of the inflow of remittances from the Gulf region, unemployed youths were unwilling to take up employment in the agricultural sector. Mention may be made in this connection that Hayami, a Japanese economist who visited Kerala was surprised to find a large number of educated youths remaining idle rather than taking up agricultural occupations.[32] Needless to say, natives of other parts of India take advantage of the situation and pour into Kerala for taking up various occupations despised by the Malayalees. They are even prepared to work for more hours at lower rates of wages.

Inmigration to Kerala is to some extent similar to the situation in the Punjab. While most of the works related to agriculture are being performed by the inmigrants from other parts of India, Punjabis opt themselves to emigrate to foreign lands. Similarly, various kinds of works which Keralites are reluctant perform are being taken up by the people from other parts of India. However, the incidence of unemployment is very low in Punjab against high rates in Kerala. Nevertheless in both cases, inmigration is linked with the inflow of remittances arising from the emigration of the sons of the soil to distant lands.

Notes and References

1. Anstey, Vera: *The Economic Development of India* (London, Longman Green & Co., 1936), p. 488.
2. G.O.I. *Review of Trade of India* (Calcutta, Government Press, 1932).
3. Anstey, Vera: *op.cit.*
4. K.C. Zachariah: *A Historical Study of Internal Migration in the Indian Sub-Continent 1901-1931* (Bombay, Asia Publishing House, 1964), p. 5.
5. Iyer, Subramaniam, G., *Some Economic Aspects of British Rule in India* (Madras, Swadeshi Mitran Press, 1903), p. 193.
6. Timberg, Thomas A., *The Marwaris from Traders to Industrialists* (New Delhi, Vikas Publishing House, 1978), p. 62.
7. K.C. Zachariah: *op.cit.*, p. 215.
8. Davis, Kingsley: *The Population of India and Pakistan* (New Jersey, Princeton University Press, 1951), p. 118.
9. Davis, Kingsley: *op.cit.*, p. 118.
10. Davis, Kingsley: *op.cit.*, p. 120.
11. Government of the Princely State of Travancore: *Report of the Unemployment Enquiry Committee 1928* (Trivandrum, Government Press), p. 21.
12. *Report of the Unemployment Enquiry Committee 1928 op cit.* P.44.
13. *Report of the Administration of Travancore 1942-43* (Trivandrum, Government Press, 1943), p. 11.
14. K.C. Zachariah: "Migration and Population Growth in Kerala: in R.S. Kurup (ed.), *Population Growth in Kerala* (Trivandrum, Demographic Research Centre Bureau of Economics and Statistics, Government of Kerala, 1965), p. 109.
15. K.V. Joseph: *Migration and Economic Development of Kerala* (Delhi, Mittal Publications, 1988), p. 52.
16. Government of Madras: *Report of the Tenancy Committee 1940*, p.15.
17. *Census of Madras 1931, Part I*, Report, p. 82.
18. *Census of Madras 1901, Imperial Tables.*
19. Lewandowski, Susan: *Migration and Ethnicity in Urban India, Kerala Migrants in the City of Madras* (New Delhi, Manohar 1980), p. 82.
20. *Census of Mysore 1951, Part I Report*, p. 187.
21. Lewandowski, Susan; *op.cit.* p. 192.
22. K.V. Joseph: *op.cit.*, pp.53-54.
23. *Census of Madras 1951, Census Handbook Malabar District*, pp. 246-247.
24. K.V. Joseph: *op.cit.*, p. 106.
25. Davis, Kingsley, *op.cit.*, p. 120.
26. K.V. Joseph: *op.cit.*, p. 106.
27. K.C. Zachariah et.al. *Impact of Migration on Kerala's Economy and Society* (Working Paper No.297, Trivandrum, Centre for Development Studies, 1999), pp.8-9.
28. Government of India, *Census of India 1961, Vol.I, Part II, C.IV*, Migration Table.

29. Government of India: *Census of India 1991, Vol.I, Part II D, Series Migration Tables*.
30. The number of job seekers in the state as per the rolls of the employment exchanges exceeded 33 lakhs in 1990. The number has been progressively increasing every year and in 1999, the number totalled 87.90 lakhs (See Government of Kerala, *Economic Review 1999*, Trivandrum, State Planning Board).
31. Government of Travancore: *Report of the Unemployment Enquiry Committee of Travancore 1928* (Trivandrum, Government Press).
32. K.V. Joseph, *Culture and Industrial Development: The Indian Experience* (New Delhi, Anmol Publications, 2004), p. 153.

Chapter 5

Socio-Economic and Demographic Profile of the Migrants

Migrants as an author puts, are not the random selection of the population of a given area of land.[1] Not all categories of people opt to migrate. What categories of people are involved in the process of migration and what exactly are their profile are important questions posed in any study on migration. Indicators like the educational qualification, linguistic profile, age composition, sex-ratio, rural-urban origin of the migrants and so on form important components of the profile of the migrants. The sections that follow contain a brief account of the socio-economic and demographic profile of the migrants from Kerala.

Educational Profile

Most of the migrants who moved from India during the nineteenth century were labourers recruited under indenture system. They were uneducated people from the rural areas. Only towards the closing decades of the nineteenth century other categories of migrants began to move from India. During the nineteenth century migrants from Kerala were very few. Naturally, labour migration under indenture was practically nil from Kerala. Migration from Kerala became brisk only after the spread of education. The migrants who moved from Kerala to Malaya, Burma or Ceylon were better educated people though some labour migrants were also included among them.

The educational profile of the outmigrants from Kerala was more or less similar to that of the emigrants to foreign lands. However, the migrants from Travancore and Cochin had an edge in their educational profile over those from Malabar. A survey was made in Cochin during the 1931 Census to collect information about the educational profile of the migrants. The various categories of migrants were as given in Table 5.1.[2]

Table 5.1: Educational Profile of the Migrants from Cochin in 1931*

Sl. No.	*Level of Education*	*Males*	*Females*	*Total*
1.	I.C.S., F.C.S. etc.	6	—	6
2.	Legal Profession	77	—	77
3.	Medical Profession including Veterinary	103	8	111
4.	Engineering	94	—	94
5.	Graduates and Post graduates	261	25	286
6.	Intermediate	222	16	238
7.	Mechanics, Technicians, Craftsmen etc.	191	2	193
8.	Matriculate	1112	45	1157
9.	Below Matriculation	28641	8939	37580
	Total	30707	9035	39742

Source: *Census of Cochin, 1931;Special Migration Tables.*
(Note: *The figures do not tally with the migration tables based on birth place)

As indicated in the Table, migrants included highly educated persons consisting of both males and females. There were I.C.S. officers, engineers, doctors, lawyers, post-graduates, graduates and a number of personnels with technical skill in various trades and crafts. Nevertheless, the ranks of the migrants also included those with lesser qualification. Migrants from other regions of Kerala also included highly qualified persons; though the data on such details are scanty. Interestingly, one of the earliest and prominent migrants from the former princely state of Travancore was Dr. Palpu who migrated to the then princely state of Mysore as far back as 1891. On the completion of his medical education in Madras he was denied a job in the then Travancore state as he belonged to the backward Ezhava community. He was able to secure an assignment in the medical department of the then Mysore state where he served subsequently for a number of years.[3] Similarly it was the educated youngsters from the then Malabar district who migrated to Madras city during the closing decades of nineteenth century. However, the migrants from Malabar also included fairly large number of illiterate and uneducated class of people. Most of such migrants worked in the coffee estates in Coorg, Hassan, Nilgiris etc. Some of the Muslims among them worked as hawkers in various parts of Mysore state and Madras presidency and as miners in the Kolar gold fields.[4]

As more and more young men came out of the schools and colleges the ranks of the educated persons among the migrants from Kerala swelled over the years. It was the "growing aspiration of the cultivating class for literacy and quasi literacy occupations" which motivated the educated youth to move in large numbers to other parts of India.[5] Increasing numbers of such men continued to migrate from different parts of Kerala. The Census Report of 1951 contains an interesting paper on the educational qualifications of the working population of Calcutta hailing from different parts of India. The number of such working persons from Travancore-Cochin in Calcutta Industrial Region with different levels of educational qualification was as given in Table 5.2.

Table 5.2: Educational Profile of the Migrants from Travancore-Cochin in Calcutta Industrial Region

Sl. No.	*Level of Education*	*No. of Males*	*No. of Females*	*Total*
1.	Illiterates	10	2	12
2.	Literate with no formal education	35	2	37
3.	Non-matrics	5	—	5
4.	Matrics	22	1	23
5.	Undergraduates	11	—	11
6.	Graduates	14	1	15
7.	Post-graduates	5	—	5
	Total	102	6	108

Source: *Census of India, 1951, Paper No.6, Working Population in Calcutta Industrial Region: Distribution by Industry, Place of Birth and Educational Attainment* (Calcutta, 1956).

As can be seen from the Table 5.2, most of the migrants from Travancore-Cochin were highly educated people, illiterates being very few. There were 15 graduates and 5 post-graduates out of a total of 108 persons. The number of persons holding educational qualification at matriculation or above totalled half of the migrants.

The migrants to the other parts of India would have been equally educated. As years went, the educational qualification of the migrants also improved. Table 5.3 indicates the number of migrants from Keala with different levels of educational qualification in Madras in 1961.[7]

As can be seen, most of the migrants were educated people. Illiterates accounted for only 15.79 per cent of the males and 27.67 per cent of the females. On the other hand, matriculates formed 23.70 per cent of the males and 14.81 per cent of the females. Degree holders accounted for 6.78 per cent of the males and 2.23 per cent of the females. The ranks of migrants included fairly large number of engineers, medical graduates and other categories of educated persons. The educational profile of the migrants was in fact better than that of the people at large in Kerala. The percentage of illiterates among non-agricultural workers was as high as 23.43 in the case of males and 57.85 in the case of females in Kerala as a whole.[8] The proportion of different categories of educated persons was lower in Kerala in comparison to that of the migrants from Kerala. In the case of matriculates for example, the percentage was only 9.87 in the case of female workers.

Table 5.3: Educational Qualification of the Migrants from Kerala in Madras in 1961

Sl. No.	*Level of Education*	*No. of Males*	*No. of Females*	*Total*
1.	Illiterates	5694	5340	11034
2.	Literate without formal education	9161	4754	13915
3.	Primary	9974	5779	15753
4.	Matrics	8657	2289	11516
5.	Diploma	257	14	271
6.	Degree	2477	432	2909
7.	Engineering Degree	141	—	141
8.	Medicine	109	49	158
9.	Teaching Degree	37	68	105
10.	Others	16	—	16
	Total	36523	19295	55818

Source: *Census of India 1961*, Vol.IX Madras. Part V(II) *Sepcial Migration Tables*, Table 3, Migrants classified by Education, age group etc.)

The educational profile of the migrants from Kerala was much better than that of the migrants from other parts of India (see Table 5.4).[9]

The Table indicates the educational profile of the migrants from various parts of India. Illiterates among the migrants from all the states accounted for 22.82 per cent in the case of males and 47.48 per cent in the case of females. While the percentage of illiterates from Kerala was far below the all India average, the percentage of all categories of literate persons from Kerala was much higher than the all India average and that of the other states except in the case of technical degree holders. In the case of different categories of educated persons among the females also the percentage of migrant females from Kerala was higher than that of all other states. Needless to say, the profile of migrants in respect of educational qualification was superior to that of the migrants from other states.

The profile of the migrants from Kerala to Bombay was also superior

Table 5.4: Distribution of the Migrants on the Basis of Educational Qualification from various States to Madras City in 1961

Sl. No.	Level of Educational Qualification	Percentage of Migrants from Kerala		Andhra Pradesh		Karnataka		Others		Average of all	
		Males	*Females*	*Males*	*Females*	*Males*	*Females*	*Males*	*Females*	*Males*	*Females*
1.	Illitrates	15.49	27.83	25.08	46.90	17.51	33.06	22.12	42.24	22.82	47.48
2.	Literate with no formal education	25.08	24.63	21.70	21.61	23.51	26.18	26.42	24.55	24.42	20.87
3.	Primary	27.3	29.95	23.08	23.38	25.20	28.71	25.70	24.04	25.21	23.10
4.	Secondary	23.70	14.81	21.29	6.96	23.24	11.39	18.76	7.40	20.73	7.38
5.	Diploma (Technical & non-technical	0.70	0.08	0.88	0.04	1.33	0.10	0.65	0.62	0.64	0.03
6.	Degree	6.78	2.23	6.18	1.07	7.03	2.19	5.40	1.39	5.38	0.87
7.	Technical Degree	0 58	0.43	0.59	0.02	2.18	0.40	0.93	0.30	0.87	0.02
	Total	100.00	100.00	100.00	100.00	100.00	100.00	100.00	100.00	100.00	100.00

Source: *Census of India 1961*, Vol. IX, Madras, Part X(II) Sepcial Migration Tables, Madras City, Table 3, Migrants Classified by Age, Sex, Educational Standards etc.

in comparison to the migrants from other parts of India in the case of all categories of educated persons as Tables 5.5 and 5.6 illustrate.[10]

In fact, the educational profile of the migrants from Kerala to Bombay was even better than that of the migrants to Madras. Illiterate males formed 11 per cent of the migrants from Kerala. It was 18 per cent in the case of female migrants from Kerala. In respect of all other categories, the educational profile of the migrants from Kerala was superior. Matriculates formed 32.67 per cent of the total male migrants from Kerala. Profile of female migrants was even superior. The percentage of degree holders among the female migrants from Kerala was 10.34 and the percentage of matriculates was 42.91 per cent. The percentage of degree holders was higher only in the case of the migrants from West Bengal. Migrants from no other state came anywhere near to that of the migrants from Kerala in educational qualifications.

Zachariah has prepared an index of the educational attainment of the working migrants in Bombay for the year 1961. The average for the country as a whole was 4.19 in the case of males and 2.97 in the case of females. With an index of 7.13 for males and 7.89 for females, migrants from Kerala topped the list among the states in India in respect of the indices of educational attainment. West Bengal came second and Andhra Pradesh at the bottom in the ranking of index of educational attainment among various states.[11] Only foreign migrants from Pakistan were above the migrants from Kerala in the gradation of the index of educational attainment.

The percentage distribution of the migrants from various states in respect of each category of educational qualification has also been calculated by Zachariah. Male migrant workers from Kerala formed 3.35 per cent and females 2.54 per cent respectively of the total migrant workers. As a ratio to the total illiterate migrants workers in the country, male workers from Kerala formed 1.2 per cent and females migrant workers from Kerala 0.73 per cent. Needless to say, illiterate migrant workers from Kerala formed only a tiny proportion of the total.[12] On the other hand, as a ratio to the total number of matriculates and degree holders the percentages of male migrants from Kerala were 9.86 and 7.62 respectively. In the case of females, the percentages were respectively 9.73 and 4.72. The percentages were higher than that of Kerala only in respect of the migrants from Gujarat and Karnataka.

The educational profile of the migrants from Kerala has recorded further improvement in course of time (see Table 5.7).[13] While the percentage of illiterates has declined the percentage of all other categories of educated persons has recorded further improvement.

Table 5.5: Educational Profile of the Migrants (Males) in Bombay from Various States in 1961 (percentage)

Sl. No.	*Name of the State*	*Illiterates*	*Literates with no formal education*	*Primary level of education*	*Matriculation*	*Techinial Diploma*	*Degree (Technical and non-technical*
1.	Maharashtra	34.81	27.32	28.04	7.72	0.26	2.28
2.	Gujarat	16.96	25.17	36.28	14.75	0.54	6.26
3.	Uttar Pradesh	48.36	28.16	16.83	4.67	0.16	1.29
4.	Karnataka	22.64	27.18	24.72	17.77	0.88	6.95
5.	Rajasthan	24.14	30.96	24.84	14.47	0.59	4.97
6.	Andhra Pradesh	57.54	24.16	10.65	4.68	0.46	2.48
7.	Tamil Nadu	27.05	28.73	20.28	16.70	0.78	6.43
8.	Goa	14.48	32.80	27.42	16.46	0.63	4.18
9.	Kerala	11.45	22.50	23.63	32.67	0.89	8.83
10.	Madhya Pradesh	20.70	25.37	27.01	16.83	1.49	8.56
11.	West Bengal, Assam and Orissa	19.27	25.08	22.88	20.58	1.71	9.90
12.	All India (average)	31.90	27.07	25.61	11.08	0.43	3.86

Source: Census of India 1961, Part X (IC) *Greater Bombay Special Migraiton Tables.*

Table 5.6: Educational Profile of the Migrants (Females) in Bombay from Various States in 1961 (percentage)

Sl. No.	*Name of the State*	*Illiterates*	*Literates with no formal education*	*Primary level of education*	*Matricu-lation*	*Techinial Diploma*	*Degree (Technical and non-technical*
1.	Maharashtra	77.30	4.95	6.29	7.21	0.43	3.97
2.	Gujarat	60.11	9.12	9.89	8.83	2.24	9.72
3.	Uttar Pradesh	50.34	16.89	11.84	12.93	1.61	6.35
4.	Karnataka	48.10	16.50	12.30	16.07	0.63	5.61
5.	Rajasthan	50.56	10.35	9.30	17.35	1.76	10.67
6.	Andhra Pradesh	80.53	8.29	6.54	3.46	0.27	0.89
7.	Tamil Nadu	51.83	12.14	12.36	15.25	2.42	5.96
8.	Goa	52.55	18.49	11.95	13.25	0.64	3.09
9.	Kerala	18.59	12.54	10.03	42.91	5.57	10.34
10.	Madhya Pradesh	21.54	13.70	21.93	25.45	4.17	13.18
11.	West Bengal, Assam and Orissa	14.88	12.96	14.81	28.93	1.85	15.04
12.	All India (average)	64.77	8.78	8.65	11.19	1.03	5.55

Source: *Census of India 1961*, Part X (IC) *Greater Bombay Special Migraiton Tables*.

Table 5.7: Distribution of the Migrants from Kerala in the Important Cities of India in 1971 on the Basis of Educational Qualification (Percentage)

Sl.No.	*Level of Education*	*Delhi*		*Bombay*		*Bangalore*		*Madras*	
		Males	*Females*	*Males*	*Females*	*Males*	*Females*	*Males*	*Females*
1.	Illiterates	9.54	14.17	11.11	16.90	13.33	19.27	11.93	23.03
2.	Literate with no formal education	7.95	8.26	6.25	6.96	6.77	7.63	11.05	11.62
3.	Primary education	8.38	8.90	17.91	14.15	19.16	16.86	18.15	20.14
4.	Middle School	8.99	10.14	17.57	18.62	17.88	18.55	18.70	17.25
5.	Matriculation	39.18	46.17	30.22	36.11	35.64	33.34	35.56	25.63
6.	Diploma	1.20	0.18	1.88	1.97	1.27	0.56	1.05	0.07
7.	Graduates and Postgraduates	21.75	9.46	7.92	4.18	4.75	2.92	2.98	1.51
8.	Technical Degree including education	2.54	2.16	1.07	1.07	0.86	0.67	0.84	0.07
	Total	100.00	100.00	100.00	100.00	100.00	100.00	100.00	100.00

Source: *Census of India 1971 - Migration Tables* D.3, Migrants to Urban Centres having 100,000 and above population classified by sex, educational level etc.

There was however slight fall in the percentage of females in respect of matriculates and graduates. Certain regional variations are discernible in the distribution of different categories of educated persons from place to place. The proportion of matrics and above are higher in Delhi followed by Bombay, Bangalore and Madras in the descending order. The educational profile of the migrants would have recorded further improvement since 1970s, though the data on the same are scanty.

Age Composition of the Migrants

The age composition of the migrants form another key element in the profile of the migrants. Very young children can move to another place only if their parents migrate. On the other hand, old people may not be inclined to move to other places. That leaves the young people as the only class inclined to migrate. At the same time, youngsters are in a position to adjust themselves smoothly in a new environment. Furthermore, it is the youngsters who would be in the look out for employment in distant lands. Naturally, young people would form the bulk of the migrants in any migratory stream.

We shall now examine how far this general pattern is relevant in the case of the migrants from Kerala. Table 5.8 and 5.9 indicates the age composition of the migrants from Kerala.[14]

As can be seen from Table 5.8 young children upto the age of 14 were very few among the male migrants from Kerala though young children formed about 40 per cent of the population. Young children upto 14 years did not account even 20 per cent of the migrants. On the other hand, the percentage of the migrants from the age 15 was steadily increasing upto the age of 29 and then falling.

While the percentage of the migrants in the age group 20-24 was the highest in Tamil Nadu, Maharashtra and Karnataka, the percentage of the age group 25-29 was the highest in Delhi. The percentage varies from 28.08 in Maharashtra to 15.47 in Tamil Nadu. The percentage of the migrants in the age group 25-29 formed the second largest group in all these states except in Delhi where it formed the largest group. The percentage of the migrants in the age group 30-34 was the third from top in all the four states.

The age group 20-24 forms the most important stage in the life cycle of persons seeking employment in India. On attaining the age of 20 most of them would have completed their education and would be seeking employment. They would be sufficiently matured to seek employment in distant lands. More number of Keralites of this age

Table 5.8: Age Composition of the Migrants from Kerala Residing in Other States for the Last 9 years in 1991 (Males)

Sl. No.	*Age-group*	*Tamilnadu*	*Karnataka*	*Maharashtra*	*Delhi*
1.	0-4	5.95	5.86	6.30	4.89
2.	5-9	8.51	6.78	5.46	4.84
3.	10-14	5.72	3.33	1.82	2.84
4.	15-19	7.81	9.76	6.09	4.63
5.	20-24	15.47	22.78	28.08	21.45
6.	25-29	15.75	15.60	24.82	26.66
7.	30-34	11.52	11.08	12.59	19.84
8.	35-39	9.98	7.86	6.33	7.85
9.	40-44	5.94	6.04	2.89	3.75
10.	45-49	4.69	3.58	1.84	2.49
11.	50-54	3.05	2.21	1.10	1.52
12.	55-59	2.09	1.48	0.54	1.07
13.	60-64	1.73	1.16	0.43	0.63
14.	65-69	1.74	0.79	0.28	0.37
15.	70-75	0.18	0.52	0.10	0.28
16.	76+	0.86	0.52	0.39	0.36
17.	Age not known	0.32	0.58	0.56	0.41
18.	Total	100.00	100.00	100.00	100.00

Source:Census of India 1991, Migration Tables. Table D-16, *Migrants by Place of last residence and age for duration of residences of 0-9 years.*

group would be seeking jobs in distant lands as the incidence of unemployment among the educated is stated to be very high in Kerala. No wonder, the percentage of migrants under this age group was the highest from Kerala. The age group 25-29 which sends the second largest number of migrants from Kerala is also composed of those endowed with potentialities for sending large number of migrants. Naturally, the number of migrants under this age group would be pretty high. The age group 30-34 forms the third ranking group in respect of the number of migrants. Some of the migrants under this age group would be seeking jobs with better prospects in distant lands or some others would be from the ranks of unemployed.

The age composition of the female migrants from Kerala corresponds to that of the male migrants with minor variations. If the main motive for migration with the males is believed to be employment, the main motive for females is marriage. The mean marriage in Kerala appears to be 27.9 for males and 22.3 for females. Some of the females also would be seeking employment. Naturally, the proportion of females in the age group 20-24 is the highest in all the four states.

Male migrants in the age groups 20-34 formed 42.74 per cent in

Table 5.9: Age Composition of the Migrants from Kerala Residing in Other State for the Last 0-9 years in 1991 (Females)

Sl. No.	*Age-group*	*Tamilnadu*	*Karnataka*	*Maharashtra*	*Delhi*
1.	0-4	5.76	6.32	6.50	4.85
2.	5-9	6.84	7.38	7.51	4.44
3.	10-14	4.36	3.19	4.42	2.56
4.	15-19	7.28	9.61	4.80	7.19
5.	20-24	22.61	24.29	22.62	27.00
6.	25-29	23.92	21.59	27.62	28.07
7.	30-34	10.07	9.88	12.97	11.43
8.	35-39	5.42	5.11	4.90	4.60
9.	40-44	2.90	2.83	2.64	2.06
10.	45-49	2.45	2.01	1.32	1.25
11.	50-54	2.22	1.79	1.03	1.02
12.	55-59	1.39	1.28	1.00	1.05
13.	60-64	1.80	1.11	1.35	0.97
14.	65-69	1.20	1.08	1.06	0.72
15.	70-75	0.52	0.84	0.41	0.40
16.	76+	1.01	0.77	1.06	0.46
17.	Age not known	0.17	-0.41	0.61	-0.40
18.	Total	100.00	100.00	100.00	100.00

Source: *Census of India 1991, Series I, India, Migration Tables*. Table D-16, *Migrants by Place of last residence and age for duration of residences of 0-9 years.*

Tamilnadu, 49.46 per cent in Karnataka, 65.49 per cent in Maharashtra and 64 per cent in Delhi. Female migrants in the same age group were 56, 58, 63.21 and 63.5 percent respectively. Apparently, migrants in the other age groups were not many in any of the states.

Linguistic Profile of the Malayalee Migrants

Migrants have invariably to move from one linguistic sector to another. Proficiency in languages other than their own mother tongue is very helpful for them to mingle and deal with the people of the host society. Since as many as 14 major languages are spoken in India, the migrants must be proficient in common languages like English or Hindi in addition to the local language of the place of destination. Naturally, the belingual proficiency of the migrants varies from place to place or region to region.

Table 5.10[15] indicates the belingual proficiency of the Malayalee migrants in different regions of the country.

As can be seen from the Table, the belingual proficiency of the migrants from Kerala varied from place to place. Though English

Table 5.10: Linguistic Profile of the Malayalees in Four Important Metropolitan Cities of India in 1961

Sl. No.	Language	Bombay	Delhi	Madras	Banglore	Average of the four cities	Average of the total Malayalees outside Kerala
1.	English	36.55	51.59	23.61	27.81	31.33	13.77
2.	Hindi	24.90	18.10	0.94	6.85	12.73	5.21
3.	Tamil	2.76	2.07	40.57	15.90	18.59	15.36
4.	Kannada	0.40	-	0.28	10.23	1.97	6.22
5.	Marathi	1.43	0.07	-	-	0.59	
6.	Telugu	0.08	-	0.24	0.62	0.23	0.74
7.	Tulu	-	-	-	-	-	6.35
8.	Other languages	2.50	0.43	0.19	2.82	2.68	1.41
	Total	58.62	72.26	65.99	64.23	67.12	48.46

Source: Census of India 1961: Cultural Tables Bilinguilism.

continues to be the link language, only 13 per cent of the Malayalee migrants are proficient in English as a subsidiary language in the country as a whole. In Bombay, Delhi and Bangalore, English was as the subsidiary language spoken by the largest percentage of Malayalee migrants. On the other hand, Tamil formed the subsidiary language of 40.59 per cent of Malayalees in Madras. In fact, the percentage of Malayalee migrants speaking Tamil as a subsidiary language in the country as a whole was 15.36; a percentage larger than the percentage of people speaking English as a subsidiary language. Higher percentage of Tamil as a subsidiary language would be due to the presence of the largest contingent of Malayalee migrants in Madras. The actual number of Malayalee migrants in Tamilnadu was 449,206 in 1961; nearly half of the total Malayalam speaking population outside Kerala. The early beginnings of migration from Kerala to Tamilnadu would be another contributory factor.

While Tamil was spoken as the subsidiary language by more number of Malayalees in Madras, Kannada, the local language of Karnataka was used as a subsidiary language by 10.23 per cent of the Malayalees in Bangalore. In fact, Tamil was used as a subsidiary language by about 15 per cent of the Malayalees in Bangalore. It could be due to the cosmopolitan character of Bangalore city where Kannada was the mother tongue of 23.7 per cent of the population in 1951 against a Tamil speaking population of 31.7 per cent.[16] Similarly, Marathi, the local language of Bombay was spoken as the subsidiary language by 1.43 per cent of the Malayalees. This could also be due to the cosmopolitan character of Bombay where only 42.8 per cent of the people spoke Marathi as their mother tongue in 1961.[17]

Significantly, Tulu was spoken as a subsidiary language by 6.35 per cent of the Malayalees living outside Kerala. As a language, Tulu is spoken as mother tongue only in South Canara district of Karnataka state. There were as many as 157,617 Malayalee migrants in South Canara in 1961. Apparently, a sizeable number of them would have even using Tulu as a subsidiary language.

Hindi, the official language of the Union Government is spoken as the mother tongue by the majority of the people in the north Indian states. However, the percentage of Malayalees using Hindi as a subsidiary language was only 5.21. Nevertheless, Hindi was the second ranking subsidiary language of the Malayalees in Bombay and Delhi.

The table illustrates that Keralites do not use any other subsidiary language on a significant scale in any part of India. In fact, only 48 per cent of the Malayalees in other regions spoke any other subsidiary language. Though Keralites are the highly educated class among the migrants in India, their linguistic profile is not very high. They would preferably attain proficiency after reaching those places. The linguistic profile of the migrants might have undergone changes since 1961.

Sex Ratio

Migration was essentially a male phenomenon for centuries in the past. In all types of migration from India, males outnumbered females from the very beginning. However, the disparity between the two has come down considerably by 1961. (See Table 5.11).

Table 5.11: Sex Composition of the Migrants from Various States (Percentage)

Sl. No.	*Name of the State*	*1961* *Males*	*Females*	*1991* *Males*	*Females*
1.	Andhra Pradesh	49.71	50.29	41.99	58.01
2.	Assam	37.39	52.61	48.56	51.44
3.	Bihar	63.75	36.25	53.33	46.67
4.	Gujarat	54.81	45.19	44.27	55.73
5.	Haryana			31.73	68.27
6.	Himachal Pradesh	49.71	50.29	45.06	54.94
7.	Jammu and Kashimir	63.48	36.52	44.63	55.37
8.	Karnataka	46.07	53.93	40.14	59.86
9.	Kerala	64.88	35,12	52.49	47.51
10.	Madhya Pradesh	37.74	62.26	42.89	57.11
11.	Maharashtra	45.71	54.29	36.17	63.82
12.	Orissa	57.56	42.44	45.61	64.39
13.	Punjab	51.97	42.03	43.44	56.56
14.	Rajasthan	48.16	51.84	39.96	60.04
15.	Tamil Nadu	52.66	47.4	49.11	50.89
16.	Uttar Pradesh	60.56	39.44	52.19	47.81
17.	West Bengal	45.63	54.37	37.30	63.70
18.	Delhi	39.95	60.05	28.55	71.15
19.	Others	—	—	—	—
20.	All India	53.70	47.30	45.53	54.47

Source: (1) *Census of India 1961, Vol.I, Part IIC, Migration Tables.*
(2) *Census of India 1991, Series I, India, Part V, D Series, D-1 Population Classified by Place of Birth*

Note: Haryana formed part of Punjab in 1961.

As can be seen from the Table, males formed 53.7 per cent of the migrants from the country as a whole in 1961. However, female ratio has been higher than that of the males in respect of the migrants from Andhra Pradesh, Madhya Pradesh, Maharashtra, Rajasthan, West Bengal,

New Delhi. The high female ratio was stated to be due to the migration of females with marriage. The male migrants numbered more than the female migrants in all the other states. In this aspect Kerala topped the list with a male migrant ratio of 64.8 per cent in 1961.

In this connection, the question is why has males outnumbered females with such wide variation in the case of migrants from Kerala? The belated entry of Kerala as an outmigrating state would have been one of the main reasons for the higher ratio of the males among the migrants from Kerala. Women migrants would be ready to move to distant lands in large numbers only after a sense of security and safety has been created by opening networks. Till then women migrants would be far less than the males. The migrants who moved from Kerala during the early decades of 20th century were in fact mere pioneers in the whole process of migration.

Since 1961 the male ratio among the migrants has been on a declining trend. As the Table indicates female outmigrants outnumbered males by 1991 and the male ratio fell below 50 per cent in the country as a whole. The number of female migrants exceeded the males in all the states expect Bihar, Assam and Kerala. There was an actual fall in the ratio of the male migrants from Kerala to 53 per cent in 1991 from 64 per cent in 1961.

Furthermore, another peculiar development became conspicuous by 1991. Though male migrants from Kerala accounted for more than half of the total from Kerala as a whole females outnumbered males in a few states (see Table 5.12).

It can be seen from the Table that the female migrants from Kerala accounted for more than 50 per cent of that of the migrants in Bihar, Madhya Pradesh, Punjab, Rajasthan, Tamil Nadu and Uttar Pradesh. In this context the question posed is, how could such a situation emerge in the case of migrants from Kerala? None of these states are noted for high level of industrial activity. However, Kerala is reputed for sending fairly large number of female para-medical professionals and nurses. It is reported that no hospital in north India can be found without the presence of a nurse from Kerala. The high female ratio among the migrants from Kerala would be due to the influx of large number of such para- medical professionals like that of nurses of Kerala origin in these states.

Rural-Urban Origin of the Migrants

According to Ravenstein propensity to migrate will be more with the people of the rural areas in comparison with the urban population.

Table 5.12: Sex Composition of the Migrants from Kerala in Various States

Sl.No.	*Name of the State*	*Males*	*Females*
1.	Andhra Pradesh	56.32	43.68
2.	Assam	54.35	45.65
3.	Bihar	47.15	52.85
4.	Gujarat	59.81	40.19
5.	Haryana	56.97	43.03
6.	Himachal Pradesh	59.27	40.73
7.	Jammu and Kashimir	—	—
8.	Karnataka	53.16	46.84
9.	Kerala	—	—
10.	Madhya Pradesh	48.92	51.08
11.	Maharashtra	59.13	40.87
12.	Orissa	56.13	43.87
13.	Punjab	39.65	60.35
14.	Rajasthan	48.12	51.88
15.	Tamil Nadu	47.99	52.01
16.	Uttar Pradesh	43.85	56.15
17.	West Bengal	54.27	45.73
18.	Delhi	52.63	43.37
19.	All India	52.49	47.51

Source: *Census of India 1991, Series I, India Part V D Series D-1 Population Classified by Place of Birth.*

The pattern in India has not been on the lines contemplated by Ravenstein. Instead propensity to migrate has been stronger with the urban population in India.

As can be seen from the Table, migrants from the urban areas formed 29 per cent and from the rural areas 71 per cent in 1961. However, urban population in the country as a whole accounted for only 18 per cent of the total population in 1961. Apparently the proportion of the migrants from the urban areas has been much higher than that of the rural areas.

By 1991, migrants from urban areas accounted for 37.17 per cent of the total, though urban population of the country as a whole was only 25.72 per cent. Bihar and Orissa were the only two states from where proportionately large number of migrants hailed from the rural areas. More than 64 per cent of the migrants hailed from the urban areas of Maharashtra.

Migrants from the urban areas of Kerala had a clear lead over migrants from rural areas in proportionate terms. Migrants from the urban areas formed 41 per cent, though urban population of the country accounted for only 18 per cent. The proportion of migrants from the urban areas went on increasing further since then. By 1991, migrants of

Table 5.13: Classification of the Migrants on the Basis of Rural/Urban Origin

Sl. No.	*Name of the State*	*1961 Rural*	*Urban*	*1991 Rural*	*Urban*
1.	Andhra Pradesh	69.96	30.04	60.49	39.51
2.	Assam	68.19	31.38	62.82	33.28
3.	Bihar	87.52	12.48	76.83	23.17
4.	Gujarat	52.33	47.67	57.31	32.69
5.	Haryana	—	—	69.02	30.98
6.	Himachal Pradesh	83.21	16.79	67.28	32.72
7.	Jammu and Kashimir	59.09	40.56	38.82	61.18
8.	Karnataka	60.18	39.82	59.93	40.07
9.	Kerala	58.76	41.24	49.38	50.62
10.	Madhya Pradesh	72.88	26.90	68.71	31.29
11.	Maharashtra	58.71	40.64	35.69	64.31
12.	Orissa	86.69	13.31	77.66	22.34
13.	Punjab	69.84	30.16	56.80	43.82
14.	Rajasthan	74.13	25.87	69.62	30.38
15.	Tamil Nadu	63.87	35.66	45.33	54.67
16.	Uttar Pradesh	73.87	25.85	68.88	31.12
17.	West Bengal	64.08	35.60	50.71	49.29
18.	Delhi	32.56	67.22	20.06	79.94
19.	Others	NA	—	—	—
20.	All India	69.79	29.12	62.87	37.17

Source: (1) *Census of India 1961, Vol.I, Part IIC, Migration Tables.*
(3) *Census of India 1991, Series I, India, Part V, D Series, D-1 Population Classified by Place of Birth*

Note: Haryana formed part of Punjab in 1961.

urban origin accounted for 51 per cent of the total migrants, though urban areas accounted for hardly 26 per cent of the state population. The clear lead of urban population in the migratory movement could be due to better transport and communication facilitates available in the urban areas.

Conclusion

In brief, the migrants from Kerala are better educated than their counterparts in other parts of India. Nevertheless the ranks of the migrants included socially and educationally backward class of people also. Majority of the migrants from Kerala are young men belonging to the labour force. Apparently, the urge for improving the economic prospects would be stronger with the migrants from Kerala. There has been a steady increase in the number of female migrants with the females outnumbering the males in many states by 1991. Majority of the migrants from Kerala are proficient in languages other than Malayalam. Propensity for migration has been stronger with the urban population of Kerala. How the migrants from Kerala endowed with the aforesaid characteristics settled down in other parts of India forms the theme of the next chapter.

Notes and References

1. King, Rusell: *The New Geography of European Migration* (London, Belhaven Press, 1993) p. 27.
2. Government of the Princely State of Cochin: *Census of Cochin 1931.*
3. Jeffrey, Robin, *Decline of Nayar Dominance* (New Delhi, Vikas Publishing House Pvt. Ltd. 1976), p. 144.
4. Government of India: *Census of India 1941, Vol.VXII: Mysore, Part I Report*, p. 24.
5. Government of the Princely State of Travancore: *Report of the Unemployment Committee 1928*, see pp. 7-10.
6. Govt. of India: *Census of India 1951*, Paper 6, *Working Population of Calcutta Industrial Region by Industry, Place of Birth and Educational Attainment.*
7. Govt. of India: *Census of India 1961, Vol.IX*, Madras Part V(II), *Special Migration Tables.*
8. Govt. of India: *Census of India 1961*, Vol , *Kerala Economic Tables.*
9. Govt. of India: *Census of India 1961*, Vol.IX, Madras, *op.cit.*
10. Govt. of India: Part X I.C. Greater Bombay, *Special Migration Tables.*
11. K.C. Zachariah: *Migration in Greater Bombay*, Bombay Demographic Research Centre, 1968, p.
12. K.C. Zachariah: *op.cit.*, p.
13. Govt. of India: *Census of India 1971 Migration Tables, D.3, Migration to Urban Centres having 100,000 and above population.*
14. Govt. of India: *Census of India 1981, Series I, India, Part V A&B (viii) Migration Tables*, Tale d.15, Migrants by Place of Last Residence and Age for Duration of Residents of 0-9 years.
15. Govt. of India: *Census of India 1961, Cultural Tables*, Bilingualism.
16. Weiner Myron: *Sons of the Soil: Migration and Ethnic Conflict in India*, New Jersey, 1978), p. 54.
17. *Ibid.*

Chapter 6

Malayalee Settlers in Other Parts of India

Introduction

In the previous chapters we have examined how the process of migration had its beginnings in Kerala and the trends in the various patterns which ensued subsequently. Within the span of one century Malayalees have emerged as a globalised community whose sons are found in almost all parts of the world. They could make a name for themselves in whichever places they have set foot.

One of the key issues in any migration study relates to what happens to the migrant in the place or places of destination. It can lead to different possibilities. One possibility for the migrant is to return to his place of origin. As an alternative he can eventually settle down in the place of destination. However, either of these alternatives are beset with a number of problems to be surmounted because the migrant moves to a place with an altogether different environment. He is in the midst of alien people living in an altogether different cultural and social set up. He can thrive in the new place, if he is prepared to adjust and adapt to the conditions of the new environment. The problems of adjustment vary from place to place. At the same time,the main purpose of the migration itself is to improve his economic prospects by taking advantage of the opportunities available in the new place. The opportunities for improving his economic prospects and the nature of the activities he will have to undertake will be different from those that he was pursuing hitherto. The attitude of the host society to the newcomer is also unknown. In such conditions how he adjusts, settles and maintains himself in the new environment are the main issues.

In order to uncover such issues Prof. Piore has formulated a theoretical model of settlement process in the context of the immigration of industrial workers in the U.S. As a starting point he regards all the migrants as transient workers. They will be prepared to accept occupations of lower status in the place of destination. They may not mind to hold on to such occupations so long as the work fetches an income and in this respect their behaviour is like that of "an economic man". In the words of Piore, "they are a group of people divorced from a social setting, operating outside the constraints and inhibitions that it imposes, working totally and exclusively for money."[1] Such behavioural pattern on the part of the migrant will be in force so long as migration remains as a mere temporary phenomenon. However, migration does not remain as a temporary phenomenon for ever. Instead, "a nucleus of more or less permanent migrants seems inevitably to grow up" in course of time.[2] At least a few migrants manage to settle down even in the cases of temporary migration like that of the labour migration in the Gulf region. Such changes are inevitable because "the radical individualism that characterizes migrant behaviour in the very early stages, which underlies the conventional economic theory of man, is essentially not a human condition. People do not live naturally so totally divorced from social ties and a structured set of community relationships and they do not live long together without the rudiments of such a structure developing".[3]

The migrants who have been initially mere sojourners in the place of destination adopt a course of action, similar in nature, apparently on account of their inability to maintain an ascetic existence for ever. Instead they bring their wives and children or relatives from their homes. Eventually, they will change their life style and will be in the look out for better jobs. They may cultivate a status consciousness along with an interest in the long run earning prospects. Such changes in the attitude and behaviour of the migrants form what he terms as settlement process.[4] Changes in the behaviour can result in a direct conflict with the sons of the soil. The difficulties and tensions of the process of settlement will be more serious in the case of migrants belonging the first generation as they are a class of outsiders. The second generation will not be from outside as they are, for practical purposes, insiders born and brought up in the place of destination. While evolving their new life style in the place of settlement the migrants may land in a cultural poverty. However, settled they actually are in the new place, the migrants belonging to the first generation will continue to regard themselves as those from some other place and retain a desire to return home. The second generation may not experience such a nostalgia.

Notwithstanding the significance of the model, it is not free from defects. First, all categories of migrants will not be content with occupations lower in status. Instead, the educated and professionally qualified class among the migrants will be seeking occupations in consonance to their qualifications and social standing. Apparently, the model seems to be inappropriate in such cases of migratory movements. Second, migrants also form their own networks on account of the insecurity and sense of isolation felt by them. Such networks become handy for consolidating their position in the new environment. The model totally disregards the significance of the networks in the very process of settlement. Another issue relates to the question of identity of the migrants. In his opinion the question of identity remains as a serious issue only with the migrants in their place of origin. In his opinion status consciousness among the migrants arises as a corollary to the settlement process. On the other hand, all the migrants are highly conscious of their status and identity under all circumstances. Nevertheless, the model provides a meaningful framework for uncovering various aspects pertaining to the settlement of the migrants in the places of destination.

Migrants from Kerala who started to distant lands seem to have been mere sojourners in the beginning. Invariably most of the migrants were males who moved alone without taking with them their wives or other members of the family. The low female sex ratio is a clear indication of his aspect. Gradually some among them started to settle down in the distant lands by bringing their families. The settlement process thus started seems to have gained momentum in course of time. Significantly the intensity of settlement reckoned as a percentage of Malayalees living in other parts of India to the migrants from Kerala went up from 145 in 1961 to well over 197 by 1991. Apparenly, by 1990s the process of settlement became a fairly widespread phenomenon.

The Malayalee migrants who settled in other parts of India would have moved for different purposes. The purposes of the migrants together with the activities undertaken by them are issues having implications on the settlement process as well as the relationship with the host society. They would have faced a lot of difficulties and to tide over them would have created their own networks. The sections that follow contain, an attempt to uncover those issues relating to settlement of Malayalee migration. Section I will be focusing on the geographical distribution of the Malayalees in various parts of India. Section II deals with the purpose of migration. Occupational distribution of the migrants forms another section. Problems of settlement, attitude of the host society, network formation, questions of identity etc. form the themes of the other section.

Geographical Distribution of Malayalees in Other Parts of India

Malayalees are perhaps the only linguistic group of people in the whole of India who did not have any enclave or niche or any settlement in other parts of India in the past. On the other hand, other linguistic groups like the Marathis, the Tamils or the Telugus had their own ethnic enclaves in various parts of India for a long time in the past. Even in Kerala, niches of the Tamils, the Telugus, the Konkanis, or even of the Gujaratis were in existence for a long period. The non-existence of such enclaves was due to the absence of any migratory tradition among the Malayalees.

During the formative stages of migration most of the migrants were mere sojourners who were interested to return to their native places after earning some income. Eventually they started to settle down in those far away places. Many of them got married and brought their families to the places where they migrated and reared their siblings in those new places. The size of Malayalee population in 1991 formed roughly two times the size of the migrants. The size of population in excess of the migrants is a clear indication of the magnitude of settlement. Though they settled in almost all parts of India, the intensity of settlement would not have been uniform. The distribution Malayalee settlers in other parts of India as on 1991 has been as given in Table 6.1.

Though Malayalee migrants have settled down in almost all parts of India, the intensity of settlement reckoned as a ratio of Malayalam speaking population in other parts of India to the migrants has not been uniform. With a percentage of 329 as a ratio to the migrants, Karnataka topped the list. The other states in the descending order were Andaman and Nicobar, Tamil Nadu, West Bengal, Bihar, Maharashtra and so on. Goa, a relatively new destination of the migrants from Kerala had a fairly high intensity of settlement. With a ratio of 83 per cent, Uttar Pradesh was at the bottom in the intensity of settlement. Majority of the settlers have congregated around the urban areas in other parts of India. Nevertheless, about one third of the Malayalees have settled down in the rural areas.

Though distributed throughout India, the overwhelming majority of the settlers have congregated in Karnataka, Tamil Nadu, Maharashtra, Madhya Pradesh, Andhra Pradesh, Delhi etc. Among them Karnataka stands foremost in accommodating the largest number of Malayalees. There were as many as 757,030[5] Malayalam speaking people in Karnataka accounting for 34 per cent of the Malayalees living in other

Table 6.1: Geographical Distribution of Malayalees in Other Parts of India

Sl. No.	*Name of the State*	*Ratio of Malayalees as a percentage of migrants in 1991*	*Distribution of Malayalee Population (Percentage)*		
			Rural	*Urban*	*Total*
1.	Karnataka	329.77	19.43	14.99	34.42
2.	Tamil Nadu	185.56	10.06	20.00	30.06
3.	Maharashtra	171.59	0.95	14.53	15.48
4.	Madhya Pradesh	116.69	0.38	3.28	3.66
5.	Andhra Pradesh	130.59	0.37	2.64	3.01
6.	Delhi	142.80	0.10	2.84	2.94
7.	Gujarat	127.60	0.30	2.32	2.62
8.	Rajasthan	143.67	0.25	0.94	1.19
9.	Andaman & Nicobar Islands	269.41	0.11	0.61	0.72
10.	Bihar	174.94	0.16	0.61	0.47
11	Orissa	161.11	0.14	0.59	0.73
12	West Bengal	177.29	0.16	0.55	0.71
13	Uttar Pradesh	83.56	—	—	—
14	Goa	152.35	0.18	0.39	0.57
15	Others	—	—	—	1.83
16	Total	195.78	33.35	64.71	100.00

Source: *Census of India 1991:*
(1) Migration Tables
(2) Language Tables.

parts of India in 1991. The proximity of Karanataka to Kerala, the agreeable climate and the growing economic and industrial activities in that state would have been the promptings which induced a large number if Malayalees to settle down in Karnataka. Against the urbanward tilt of the settlers, more than half the number of ethnic Malayalees in Karnataka are found to be living in the rural areas. This is attributable to the similarity of the agro-climatic conditions of the west coast and *malnad* districts of Karnataka with that of Kerala. Most of the settlers in the rural areas are believed to be peasant farmers from the northern part of Travancore region of Kerala. The migratory movement of the peasants from Travancore had its beginning from the time of the Second World War. As stated earlier, a large number of peasants sold their properties in Travancore and proceeded to the hilly tracts of the then South Canara district and Coorg state with their families. Some of them even occupied forest lands in the districts like Shimoga of the then Mysore state. Though the encroaches were evicted from the forest lands, migration of peasants has not subsided. In fact, peasant migrants from Travancore moved to other districts like Chikmagalur, Hassan, Uttar Kannada, Mysore and so on. Some of the localities like Puttur, Shirady, Belthangady in the present Dakshina Kannada district, Somevarapet, Virajpet in Kodagu district of Karnataka state have the appearance of typical Kerala villages with farm houses surrounded by coconut groves, areca trees, coffee plants, plantains and a variety of other vegetative growth. The Syrian Catholic settlers have even established a diocese of their own in Belthangady.

Malayalees in the rural tracts also include large number of agricultural labourers, petty traders, hawkers and other category of workers. Many of them started to settle down in various parts of Karnataka state from the early decades of last century itself. In such centres, shops, provision stores, tea stalls and other petty business establishments owned by Malayalees are a regular sight. A good number among them belong to the Mappilla Muslim community of Kerala.

Notwithstanding the numerical strength of the rural settlers, urban areas also contain large number of migrant settlers from Kerala. Bangalore, the capital city of Karnataka has become a haven of migrants from Kerala since the Second World War. It was the growing industrial and business activities of Bangalore which have been instrumental in attracting Malayalees in larger numbers. Since the IT boom of the 1990s there has been an exodus of young engineers and other professionals from all over Kerala. Places like Koramangala, Madivala, Indira Nagar, Yesvantpur are the important localities where Malayalees are found in large numbers. Provision stores, restaurants, bakeries and pan shops owned by Malayalees are numerous in many parts of the city. Koshy's restaurant in Brigade road was a favourite chocie of the elite for a number of years. Urban centres like Mangalore, Mysore and Udupi have also become the abode of Malayalees of different shades.

Tamil Nadu comes second by accommodating 30 per cent non-Keralite Malayalees. Till 1970s, Tamil Nadu,was the haven of largest number of Malayalees. Even now, Tamil Nadu continues to be the destination of the largest number of outmigrants from Kerala. In fact, as stated in the previous chapters the old Madras presidency was the main destination of all categories of migrants from Kerala from the formative days of the migratory movement for various reasons.

As in the case of Karnataka, the rural areas of Tamil Nadu also contain large number of Malayalee population. Most of them are found in Nilgiri and Kanyakumari districts of Tamil Nadu. These two districts were connected with Kerala for a long period in the past. While Kanyakumari district was part of the former princely state of Travancore,

Gudalur taluk in Nilgiri district was owned by the Nilambur Kovilakom, a feudal family of Malabar district. Naturally, some Malayalees were residing in these districts for a long time in the past.[6] Their strength was reinforced by the influx of some peasant farmers from Travancore who migrated to these two districts since the Second World War. The original Malayalee inhabitants of these districts together with the peasant migrants from Travancore form the bulk of the Malayalee settlers in the rural areas of Tamil Nadu. They are peasant farmers who cultivate rubber, coconut, pepper, ginger, plantain and such other crops which are popular in Kerala. The ranks of rural settlers include agricultural labourers, estate workers, petty traders and hawkers.

As in the past, the urban areas of Tamil Nadu continue to be attractive destination to the outmigrants from Kerala. Many of them have opted to settle down in various urban centres of Tamil Nadu. Madras, renamed as Chennai, the capital city of Tamil Nadu became the abode of large number of Malayalee settlers, nicknamed as Malayalathans by the Tamilians. Some of the settlers belong to the third and fourth generation of migrants. Other towns like Coimbatore, Madurai, Tiruchirapalli, Nagarcoil and so on are also crowded with Malayalee settlers. Furthermore, many Malayalees frequent various parts of Tamil Nadu for business, education, pilgrimage and even for social functions like marriage.

Maharashtra where about 16 per cent Malayalee settlers reside holds the third ranking state of non-Keralite Malayalees. Most of them reside in the urban areas of Maharashtra. Though a few Malayalees were reported to have migrated for the purpose of pineapple cultivation, majority of the Malayalees in Maharashtra are in Mumbai, the capital city of Maharashtra state and also the financial capital of India. According to 1991 census there were as many as 173,460 Malayalam speaking population in Mumbai. They formed more than 8 per cent of the Malayalees living in other parts of India.[7] As stated earlier, Malayalees started to migrate to Bombay from the early decades of 20th century. Other cities of Maharashtra like Pune, Sholapur, Nagpur also contain sizable number of Malayalees.

Practically, almost all the settlers in other parts of India have settled down in the urban areas. Urban centres like Delhi, Ahmedabad, Hyderabad, Calcutta contain fairly large number of Malayalee settlers. In Delhi, for example, more than 3 per cent of the Malayalees living outside Kerala are stated to be residing. Even lesser populous towns like Rajkot, Surat, Kanpur, Lucknow, Chandigarh, Visakhapatnam, Ranchi also contain pockets of Malayalee settlers.

II

Purpose of Migration

As already stated in the introduction, migration of the modern period is a voluntary activity prompted by economic motives. Migrants can gain economic benefits by getting employment in the new place. They can as well start their own business enterprises. During the beginning, migrants go alone to the new places without taking other members of their families. Invariably, most of them would be unmarried youngsters in the age group of about 20-30. They may get married only after spending a few years in the new place and after securing a foothold there. Then only, they will think of brinigng their wives or setting up their families. Naturally, female migration is invariably linked with marriage. Ipso facto, marriage becomes a major purpose for the migration in the case of females. Similarly, other members of the family of the migrants move to the new place only after the head of the family has settled in the new place. Tables 6.2 and 6.3 based on the census report of 1991 give details of the purpose of migrants from Kerala to different states in India.

Table 6.2 indicates that more than 52 per cent of male migrants moved for the purpose of employment. The percentage of migrants who moved for the purpose of business was 8.18. Apparently more than 60 per cent of the migrants were motivated by economic/employment purposes. Marriage was an insignificant purpose for which only 1.44 per cent of the male migrants indicated as their purpose. Education was the purpose for 8.18 per cent of the migrants. As a matter of fact, education was the purpose for migration of a large number of Malayalees from the early decades of 20th century. Migrants whose purpose was migration of the family formed 18 per cent. They would be the dependent parents or children moving from Kerala to join the migrant's families settled in other states or the members of migrant families from one state to another state. Actually, the number of migrants whose place of last residence was Kerala was much lower than those whose birth place was in Kerala. They would have migrated from one state to another after originally migrating from Kerala. Even in such cases, economic consideration would have been the main motivating force.

The percentage of the migrants moving for the purpose of employment varied from state to state. The highest percentage of migrants moving for employment was in Delhi where more than 68 per cent of the migrants moved for employment. Curiously only 48 per cent

Table 6.2: Purpose of Migration of Keralites in 1991 (Males)

(Percentage)

Sl. No.	*Name of the State*	*Employ-ment*	*Business*	*Educa-tion*	*Family moved*	*Marriage*	*Natural Calamities*	*Others*
1.	Tamil Nadu	50.87	5.95	3.24	21.99	1.96	0.20	15.75
2.	Karnataka	48.19	9.87	1.81	23.47	1.32	0.26	15.64
3.	Maharashtra	57.29	10.51	3.19	11.69	0.65	0.11	16.53
4.	Madhya Pradesh	61.66	6.26	.84	15.46	0.97	0.08	10.90
5.	Andhra Pradesh	57.91	6.98	2.81	18.31	1.19	0.20	12.56
6.	Delhi	68.63	3.98	2.59	18.79	0.44	0.03	5.49
7.	Gujarat	48.57	22.00	2.01	12.23	1.35	—	13.80
8.	Rajasthan	63.40	6.34	2.50	14.53	1.84	—	11.36
9.	Uttar Pradesh	42.85	4.32	8.03	22.17	4.91	—	17.70
10.	Andaman & Nicobar Islands	62.59	8.12	1.30	18.50	1.00	—	13.20
11.	West Bengal	52.55	5.11	4.08	16.56	1.02	1.22	19.42
12	Goa	50.15	15.18	1.91	21.90	0.36	—	9.79
13	Bihar	63.24	2.96	2.69	15.29	3.19	—	10.73
14	Orissa	51.70	13.43	6.37	15.48	1.14	0.22	11.61
	State Average	52.62	8.18	4.03	18.37	1.44	0.16	15.24

Source: *Census of India 1991, Migration Tables, D-3 Migration by Place of Last Residence.*

Table 6.3: Purpose of Migration of Keralites in 1991 (Women)

(Percentage)

Sl. No.	Name of the State	Employ-ment	Business	Educa-tion	Family moved	Marriage	Natural Calamities	Others
1.	Tamil Nadu	8.59	1.01	2.12	28.73	42.27	0.25	14.05
2.	Karnataka	5.81	0.55	0.64	29.37	55.27	0.08	8.28
3.	Maharashtra	10.48	1.47	2.68	25.23	39.75	0.11	19.94
4.	Madhya Pradesh	14.59	1.19	3.86	27.86	40.97	0.12	11.38
5.	Andhra Pradesh	17.81	1.52	5.85	33.63	29.15	0.26	11.75
6.	Delhi	18.99	1.05	5.37	41.53	26.83	0.04	6.27
7.	Gujarat	12.70	5.68	1.66	34.29	29.31	0.02	16.28
8.	Rajasthan	34.03	2.58	6.28	27.48	23.18	0.12	16.28
9.	Uttar Pradesh	15.02	2.69	6.02	28.54	37.14	0.133	10.32
10.	Andaman & Nicobar Islands	6.05	0.48	1.15	50.75	34.42	—	7.10
11.	West Bengal	11.59	0.48	3.38	34.54	32.12	0.48	17.39
12	Goa	10.11	0.99	9.37	52.94	25.06	—	9.41
13	Bihar	18.29	0.96	1.42	18.90	44.91	0.20	5.97
14	Orissa	13.63	2.38	5.65	33.92	34.52	0.59	9.22
	State Average	10.84	1.24	3.33	28.92	41.41	0.18	14.03

Source: *Census of India 1991, Migration Tables, D-3 Migration by Place of Last Residence.*

of the male migrants migrated to Karnataka state for the purpose of employment. Nevertheless, 9.87 per cent of the migrants moved to Karnataka for the purpose of doing business. At the same time, migrants who moved to Karnataka on account of the migration of family was 23.47, being the highest percentage from Kerala. Most of them would be dependents of the migrants comprising both young children and old people moving for the purpose of settling down in Karnataka. Some of the earlier migrants to other states would be remigrating with their family members to Karnataka state. Apparenly, Karnataka has become the most sought after state for settlement of Keralites to which further reference will be made in the sections that follow. Gujarat was not a very attractive destination for employment to the Malayalee migrants as only 48.57 per cent of the migrants moved to Gujarat for that purpose. However, 22 per cent of the migrants, by far the highest per cent, migrated from Kerala for the purpose of doing business in Gujarat. Fairly large per cent of migrants moved to Maharashtra also for business purpose.

While the largest per cent of male migrants moved for the purpose of employment, the main purpose for female migration has been marriage, the percentage being 41.41. They would have migrated after getting married to the male migrants who had migrated earlier or gone to other states for marrying Malayalee migrants. In either case, marriage was incidental to the migration of those males who moved for the purpose of employment. The second largest purpose for which 28.92 per cent females migrated has been the migration of families. Migration for the purpose of employment among the females was only on a moderate scale, recording 10.84 per cent.

Marriage as the purpose was the highest among the female migrants to Karnataka followed by Tamil Nadu indicating respectively 55.27 and 47.27 per cent. Though employment was not a major purpose with female migrants it was the most important purpose for those who migrated to Rajasthan. Fairly large percentage of migrants moved to Delhi, Andhra Pradesh, Bihar, Uttar Pradesh and Madhya Pradesh for the purpose of employment. Needless to say, these states had a higher female ratio according to 1991 census.

In sum, migration from Kerala was mainly for the purpose of economic benefits. As migration gained momentum more and more migrants moved for the purpose of settlement, a fact well reflected in the higher percentage of females migrating for the purpose of marriage. Settlement was again the motive behind the migration for the purpose of migrating with the family.

III

Occupational Distribution of the Migrants

Since the main purpose for migration is to secure employment they would be taking up various occupations. Many of the females are also employed. According to 1961 census more than 80 per cent of the males and 20 per cent of the female migrants from Kerala were employed in various occupations. If so, which were the activities in which they were employed is the question.

According to the industrial classification adopted in the country, employment falls under nine activities. They can broadly be divided as those falling under agricultural, industrial and service activities, which in turn are termed as primary, secondary and tertiary sectors. The distribution of migrants falling under various industrial activities have been as given in Tables 6.4 and 6.5.

As can be seen from Table 6.4, more than 50 per cent of the male workers were employed in "other services" in the states like Assam, Andhra Pradesh, Punjab, Rajasthan, Uttar Pradesh, Orissa and Delhi. Even in states like Bihar, Gujarat, Karnataka, Madhya Pradesh, Maharashtra, Tamil Nadu and West Bengal "other services" was the single largest activity. Employment in the manufacturing industry was the second most important occupation for the migrants from Kerala, the percentage being 22.79 in the case of male workers of Kerala. Cultivation of land was the occupation of 5.57 per cent of the male migrant workers from Kerala in Karnataka where as stated earlier, peasants from Travancore had migrated. Similalry, there were a large number of estate workers from Kerala working in the coffee and cardamom estates in Coorg, Hassan and Chikmagalor districts of Karnataka. Not surprisingly, the percentage of persons employed in the category "mining, orchard and livestock etc." formed 16 per cent of the male workers from Kerala.

Occupational distribution of the females differed very much from that of the males. While work participation rate of the male migrant workers was as high as 81 per cent, female participation rate was not even half of that in the country as a whole. Labour participation rate of female migrant workers of Kerala was even less than that of the all India average. It formed only 21.24 per cent. Most of the female workers were employed in the "other services". Excepting Karnataka and Tamil Nadu, more than 80 per cent of the female participants were employed in the other services. The category "other services" in which females were employed included services like that of nurses, teachers, clerks,

Table 6.4: Occupational Distribution of the Male Migrant Workers of Kerala in Various States in 1961

Sl. No.	Name of the State	Total % of workers	Culti-vators	Agri. Labou-rers	Mining Orchards	House hold industry	Manufa-cturing industry	Cons-truc-tion	Trade	Trans-port	Others Ser-vices
1.	Andhra Pradesh	84.46	0.31	0.18	0.45	2.46	10.01	4.42	7.69	7.72	66.70
2.	Assam	85.91	2.12	0.12	6.62	0.19	5.40	2.70	3.60	3.40	75.80
3.	Bihar	75.66	0.12	-	5.30	0.66	43.45	3.48	2.63	4.84	39.65
4.	Gujarat	86.85	0.11	0.07	1.03	1.38	28.80	3.16	4.51	11.35	49.44
5.	Jammu & Kashmir	86.89	-	-	-	-	-	-	-	-	100
6.	Karnataka (Mysore)	84.04	5.57	4.26	16.91	3.26	16.25	10.35	10.62	3.43	29.30
7.	Madhya Pradesh	88.02	1.73	0.03	4.10	0.64	38.30	11.41	3.45	5.68	34.39
8.	Maharashtra	82.13	0.03	0.006	0.32	1.10	33.15	2.47	13.26	9.48	39.85
9.	Orissa	93.73	0.29	-	1.14	1.55	32.61	6.82	2.81	-	51.42
10.	Punjab	92.52	-	-	0.42	-	4.14	1.14	0.49	0.37	93.42
11.	Rajasthan	79.13	0.09	-	5.08	0.09	6.99	3.45	3.16	9.97	70.94
12.	Tamil Nadu (Madras)	78.14	1.98	1.44	7.26	3.01	20.49	2.31	13.49	7.03	42.95
13.	Uttar Padesh	81.28	1.52	1.14	0.49	0.085	4.95	2.99	2.05	1.93	84.89
14.	West Bengal	74.58	0.35	0.04	0.81	0.04	23.88	5.73	20.28	8.48	40.89
15.	Delhi	80.66	-	-	3.82	0.07	7.40	0.68	6.71	3.32	81.76
	Average in all the States	81.25	2.26	1.58	7.29	2.36	21.60	4.91	11.32	6.41	42.29

Source: Census of India 1961, Vol.I, India Part II C(IV) *Migration Tables*.

Table 6.5: Occupational Distribution of the Female Migrant Workers of Kerala in Various States in 1961

Sl. No.	*Name of the State*	*Total % of workers*	*Culti-vators*	*Agri. Labou-rers*	*Mining Orchards*	*House hold industry*	*Manufa-cturing industry*	*Cons-truc-tion*	*Trade*	*Trans-port*	*Others Ser-vices*
1.	Andhra Pradesh	15.37	3.06	1.98	0.008	5.37	1.90	1.57	2.15	2.15	81.72
2.	Assam	28.00	2.85	-	5.71	0.95	3.80	-	1.90	0.95	83.80
3.	Bihar	30.75	0.32	-	0.43	1.31	7.12	1.75	1.75	1.20	86.07
4.	Gujarat	13.35	3.70	2.94	0.36	1.47	4.04	1.06	0.73	2.94	82.72
5.	Jammu &	14.23	-	-	-	-	-	-	-	-	100
6.	Karnataka (Mysore)	32.54	21.18	12.18	36.42	3.32	4.18	1.29	1.27	0.17	19.99
7.	Madhya Pradesh	29.69	21.44	0.26	0.26	0.08	4.35	1.56	1.22	1.04	69.74
8.	Maharashtra	12.32	1.00	1.15	0.24	1.12	3.12	0.69	5.57	6.39	88.00
9.	Orissa	17.87	0.99	-	-	0.99	14.41	-	-	-	83.78
10.	Punjab	13.98	-	-	-	-	-	1.38	-	-	98.60
11.	Rajasthan	56.08	1.52	1.14	0.49	0.085	4.95	2.99	2.05	1.93	84.89
12.	Tamil Nadu (Madras)	18.77	4.75	7.18	26.14	8.96	5.32	0.88	3.04	1.43	42.26
13.	Uttar Padesh	21.26	1.04	0.69	1.04	-	0.69	-	0.35	1.39	94.75
14.	West Bengal	13.55	-	0.21	1.09	0.21	5.71	1.09	1.53	2.19	85.93
15.	Delhi	20 56	-	-	-	-	1.04	-	1.56	0.65	96.47

Source: Census of India 1961, Vol.I, India Part II C(IV) *Migration Tables*.

typists etc. Nurses from Kerala formed an important category of female workers in various parts of India. The most important category of occupation for females from Kerala in Karnataka was in mining, orchards and livestock. Interestingly, about 21 per cent of the female work participants were employed in the cultivation of land. Similarly, about 22 per cent of the female work participants were employed as cultivators of land in Madhya Pradesh. This was due to the opening of a collective farm in Madhya Pradesh in 1956 where some Keralites were settled. Significantly, factory employment was not an important acativity for female workers from Kerala. The actual number of women migrants from Kerala employed in manufacturing industry itself was only 2301 in the whole of India in 1961.

The industrial classification does not give a clear cut picture of the occupational distribution of the labour force. The occupations can be in the nature of salesmen, service personnel, industrial and transport workers, administrative officers, technicians and professionals, clerical service, etc. Occupational division of the migrants in the important cities of India under these categories as on 1971 has been given in Tables 6.6 and 6.7.

As can be seen from the Table, the most important occupation of the males has been production related works. This sector which corresponds to the secondary sector accounted for the highest percentage of male workers in all the cities except Delhi. However, the presence of females in this sector has been negligible. Very few Malayalees were employed in any of the occupations connected with agriculture in the urban areas. Almost all the other occupations fall within the ambit of service sector. Under this category clerical services occupied the top with 18.71 per cent of the males holding to various posts in this category. The competence of Malayalees in this category of occupation has been well recognised . As Myron Weiner puts, "in the employment of office personnel, such as typists, stenographers, accountants and clerks many employers prefer people from Kerala, since it has been their experience that they are reliable and efficient office workers".[8] The females accounted for 5.35 per cent of the jobs in the clerical cadre. Against this, 6.61 per cent of the females were employed in the technical and professional category of jobs. Apparently it was due to the presence of large number of nurses among the Malayalee migrants. Jobs under service activities accounted for 11.56 per cent of the male workers. In all the cities under reference Malayalee males were holding a fairly large percentage of posts in the executive and administrative cadres. Proportionately, more number of Malayalees were employed as

Table 6.6: Occupational Distribution of Migrants from Kerala as on 1971 in the Important Cities of India (Males)

(Percentage)

Sl. No.	Name of the City	Professional & technical related workers	Admin. Officer	Clerical work	Sales works	Service work	Production related works	Others	Non-worker	Total
1.	Bombay	5.98	6.53	20.72	8.78	10.26	26.75		19.78	100.00
2.	Delhi	10.33	13.58	28.34	3.49	8.50	7.63		25.07	100.00
3.	Bangalore	3.74	3.27	12.43	12.47	17.90	23.62		25.54	100.00
4.	Madras	3.02	4.28	9.87	6.62	14.71	37.53		23.32	100.00
5.	Calcutta	7.17	6.11	25.52	7.93	8.08	11.93		6.96	100.00
6.	Ahmedabad	3.47	2.00	24.29	5.20	13.21	31.24		18.69	100.00
7.	Poone	4.65	23.10	15.52	3.30	9.37	18.22		23.85	100.00
8.	Hyderabad	5.82	21.22	17.47	5.62	9.27	16.88		23.09	100.00
9.	Kanpur	4.81	56.70	8.24	0.34	—	8.24		16.49	100.00
	Average of all	5.50	7.77	18.71	8.38	11.56	24.66	1.59	21.83	100.00

Source: *Census of India 1971: Migration to Urban Units having 1,00,000 and above Population.*

Table 6.7: Occupational Distribution of Migrants from Kerala as on 1971 in Important Cities of India (Females)

(Percentage)

Sl. No.	Name of the City	Professional & technical related workers	Admin. Officer	Clerical work	Sales works	Service work	Production related works	Others	Non-worker	Total
1.	Bombay	7.78	0.06	6.58	0.13	2.56	0.70		81.91	100.00
2.	Delhi	13.14	1.01	5.58	0.30	4.31	0.13		76.11	100.00
3.	Bangalore	3.35	0.49	4.77	0.245	1.69	3.82		87.12	100.00
4.	Madras	2.09	0.14	1.94	0.28	0.43	1.44		93.57	100.00
5.	Calcutta	11.16	0.31	2.98	0.15	2.83	0.47		81.76	100.00
6.	Ahmedabad	3.71	0.30	6.50	—	0.30	0.60		87.92	100.00
7.	Poone	2.45	—	5.81	0.15	0.61	1.99		88.82	100.00
8.	Hyderabad	5.31	0.28	2.44	0.14	1.40	—		89.36	100.00
9.	Kanpur	12.50	—	1.13	—	—	—		85.22	100.00
	Average of all	6.61	0.24	5.35	0.17	2.16	0.99	0.30	85.18	100.00

Source: *Census of India 1971: Migration to Urban Units having 1,00,000 and above Population.*

administrators in all parts of India. It was primarily due to their superior profile in educational qualification. Majority of the migrants in other parts of India would have taken up occupations similar in nature except those who moved to the rural areas of Karnataka and Tamil Nadu of whom reference was made earlier. Similarly, the same pattern of occupational distribution would have continued since 1970s.

IV

Problems of Settlement

Problems of settlement arise primarily because people born and brought up in one cultural milieu will have to adjust and even adopt the customs and values of another culture. No one will be happy to give up the mode of life and values which moulded his life style and adopt new customs and values. In this connection, Weiner describes the dilemmas of migrants in a new environment in clear terms thus: "There is probably a natural preference on the part of most people to live in a locality, where they share the same languages and culture with their neighbours where their children can marry within their own ethnic community, where they can buy familiar food, read newspapers in their own mother tongue, attend a familiar temple, send their children to a school conducted in their own language and in general to avoid the discomfort and the hostility – that so often accompanies living as a stranger in an alien culture".[9] Naturally the settlement process besets with a number of problems which any migrant has to surmount.

The settlement of Malayalee migrants would be beset with a number of peculiar problems also. The settlers in different parts of India encounter problems peculiar to each region. The problems in Delhi will not be the same in Mumbai or in Chennai. The difficulties which the earlier migrants faced will not be the same which the later migrants face. By and large Malayalees are not a homogenous group. They are divided into different castes and religious communities. At the same time, those who fall under these different groups face different kinds of problems.

One of the problems which any migrant faces in a new place relates to the availability of the items of food and provisions dear to him. Usually Malayalees eat rice, vegetable curry, fish curry, *puttu, appam, dosa,* etc. as their favourite items of food. Most of these items are not normally available in north India. Even if they are available, it will be only in certain localities which may not be easily accessible to each and every one staying in different corners of a city. Those who settle down with their families may also find it difficult to secure those provisions like coconut, boiled rice, banana, coconut oil etc. which are very dear to any Malayalee. Not surprisingly, it is a common sight to see Malayalee settlers travelling in the long distance trains like the Kerala Express carrying many of these provisions whenever they go back from Kerala. Of late, there is a change in the food habits of Keralites which may ease the difficulties of the new entrants in the migration field.

Another problem which haunts them is the availability of accommodation. Accommodation is both costly and short of supply in any city. Even if available, they will be in the periphery. Many of the settlers who are not well-off are compelled to stay in ramshackle sheds and pavements on account of the paucity of accommodation. Conditions in the neighbourhood of such localities may not be very hospitable to the settlers. Excepting those to whom accommodation is provided by the employer and the high income group of migrants, the vast majority of migrants are unable to get decent accommodation.

Then comes the problem from linguistic differences. Normally migrants have to be proficient in more than one language for the purpose of communication. The problem is more serious in the case of Malayalees because their own mother tongue is of no use to them in any part of India except Kerala. In this context the contention of Gore, "that the Marathi urban migrant would have the least difficulty in settling down and adjusting to life in Bombay, the Hindi migrant would have somewhat greater difficulty and the Tamil speaking migrant would have the most difficulty in these matters",[10] holds good in the case of Malayalee migrant. The problem becomes more complicated because knowledge of Tamil, the regional language of Tamil Nadu is not useful in Delhi, or Mumbai. Similarly the regional language of Mumbai is of no use in Delhi or Bangalore. A migrant cannot be a linguist. Linguistic differences create problems in the education of children and in the interaction with the linguistic community of the place of destination. Because of these linguistic differences, migrant groups cannot freely mingle and associate with the local people.

Education of the children is perhaps the most important problem. Most of the Malayalee settlers would normally be interested to send their children to the schools where Malayalam is taught. In the metropolitan cities like Mumbai, Delhi, Chennai etc. there are some schools which teach Malayalam. However, they are totally insufficient to cater to the needs of large number of Malayalee children. At the same time, the Malayalee settlers living in the remote corners of the cities like Delhi or Mumbai or Chennai are not able to send their children to these schools. As a result of this, the upper class and middle class settlers send their children to the English medium schools. The vast majority of the settlers who cannot afford to meet the high cost needed for teaching in the English medium schools, send their children to the state aided schools which charge moderate fees. As a result of these developments, the vast majority of children are not able to read and write Malayalam. At the most, they will only be able to talk Malayalam. The second or third generation among the migrants thus become Malayalees in name only.

Yet another problem confronting the Malayalee settlers in other parts of India is in regard to the marriage of their offsprings. Most of the marriages of Malayalees are being normally arranged by the parents and the alliances are within the caste/religious community and not outside the community. Since the number of members belonging to each community in each centre/city has not grown in large numbers, alliances are invariably sought in Kerala. The high percentage of females migrating for the purpose of marriage, as mentioned in the previous chapter is a clear indication of this trend. Not only the youngsters who migrate to other parts of India, but also the second generation of the migrants seek alliance from the home community. Arrangement of marriage alliance becomes difficult for the settlers because of the spatial distance between Kerala and various parts of India.

Malayalee migrants who do not have any roots in other states easily become victims of exploitation and ill-treatment there. It is the female migrants who very often get exploited easily. A typical instance is the case of female migrants working in the fish processing factories in Gujarat. Every year, large number of females are employed in such factories on a temporary basis from August to May. Majority of them are recruited from Kerala. In 1987, there were 707 female labourers working in 14 fish processing plants in Veravel city. Some of them were in the age group 12-18 years. Haribhan B. Patel describes the pathetic conditions under which these female workers work in the fish processing units thus:

"Their work time starts from 04.00 hours and ends at late evenings between 22.00 hours to 24.00 hours. They are called as the catch arrives, that is at any time of the day or night. They have to work at 0°C or sometimes below that temperature beacause fish is perishable and it has to be processed immediately. They are not provided with woollen clothes. They are not paid for the overtime. They are deprived of their week-end leaves, sick leaves or earned leaves".

He adds further:

"Once middlemen bring these females to Veraval, they are deliberately segregated from the local society and are made immobile across various employment giving units. Many females had to quit their jobs and the city in dire consequences including extreme case of losing ones own life".[11]

The number of Keralites working under such miserable conditions is very large. Many of them are exploited and made to work under inhuman conditions. The socio-economic profiles of such exploited classes are very low. They migrate to far away places and work under inhuman conditions for the sake of survival.

Nativity Movement

The attitude of the host society is perhaps the most difficult issue which the migrant community has to face. Outsiders will not normally be given the status of the natives in any community. Their position is somewhat similar to the metics in ancient Greece. As Piore maintains very often the migrants will have to take up the occupations spurned by the natives.[12] Tension and conflict ensue when the migrants demand or acquire better types of occupations. Nevertheless, Malayalees have been holding better categories of occupations in different parts of India without encountering any hostility from the locals. As a matter of fact, there was not much opposition to migrants in various parts of India in the past. Furthermore, the constitution itself guarantees equal rights to all citizens with the right to move and settle in any part of the country.

The conditions began to change with the reorganisation of the states on linguistic lines. Till then, the provincial governments were not according any special privileges to any linguistic group as most of the states were composed of multi linguistic communities. Thus for example, the former Madras presidency was composed of Tamil, Malayalee, Kannada and Telugu speaking areas where no special importance was given to any linguistic group. Officers belonging to different linguistic groups worked in all parts of these states. With the formation of linguistic states officials belonging to different linguistic groups were given the option to select their own linguistic states. In the wake of these changes, most of the Malayalee officers opted for Kerala. At the same time, most of the state governments began to promote their own linguistic groups. There was however no open hostility towards the settlers speaking other languages.

Things began to change from mid sixties in urban centres like Mumbai where anti-migrant sentiment began to surface. In Mumbai, one regional party, called Shiv Sena with the motive to secure more privileges and opportunities for Marathis was formed. They turned against migrant communities like the Malayalees and Tamils, and started to demand for more jobs to the Marathis, the sons of the soil. Racial riots against these communities erupted in various parts of the city during the seventies of 20th century.[13]

Taking the cue from Shiv Sena, anti Malayalee sentiment began to spread in Chennai, Bangalore and Goa. Malayalee shops and establishments were attacked and looted in these places also. However, it was not so violent as it was in Mumbai. Somewhat similar to Shiv Sena, an organization known as Kannada Chaluvaligar was formed in Bangalore. However, it could not gain much support in Karnataka.[14]

Such anti-Malayalee or rather anti migrant sentiments crop up on account of what Weiner calls the rise of nativism. It is a term used in the U.S. to express strong opposition to minorities of foreign origin. In the Indian context, nativism connotes sons of the soil movement directed against ethnic inmigrants from other regions. It is some sort of regional cultural identity emerging within the Indian polity. Nativism is strong in those regions where outmigration is weak but inmigration is fairly widespread as in the states like Maharashtra, Karnataka, Assam etc. The nativists like the Shiv Senites want preference or even reservation to the natives in various fields of employment. As Weiner puts it, "nativism in India is fundamentally a protectionist movement whose tariff walls are domicile regulations for employment and whose middle class population is like an infant industry seeking protection against competitive foreign imports".[15] It is directed particularly against Malayalees and Tamils in Mumbai because most of the middle ranking occupations are held by them. The nativists want protection or reservation apparently because the local candidates are not able to compete in the labour market with the better educated Malayalee migrants.

In the wake of the nativist movement most of the state governments have adopted certain policies aimed at placating the nativists. One of them stipulates that the medium of education should be in the regional language. Such an educational policy is detrimental to the interests of the migrants. In the context of such a policy migrants are compelled to send their children to unaided English medium schools, the cost of which is very often beyond the capacity of the ordinary migrants. Domicile restrictions are imposed on various categories of occupations also. Even private enterprises are bound to appoint local candidates in various kinds of occupations. In cities like Mumbai, even housing board buildings are allotted on the basis of duration of stay. Needless to say, most of these policies are directed at restricting inmigration from other states.

Of late, the original militant vigour of nativist movement has subsided. Even then, it still persists and occasionally comes to the surface. In 2002, for example, the candidates from other states who arrived in Maharashtra for a Railway Board examination for certain jobs were threatened by the activists of the Shiv Sena and the Railway Board was compelled to cancel the examination itself. Similarly, certain workers from Bihar were brutally murdered in Assam. Such violence against inmigrants creates fear and a sense of insecurity in the minds of all categories of migrants including those from Kerala. Nevertheless, the tempo of Malayalee migration to Mumbai or Chennai or Bangalore has not subsided. Instead, the magnitude of Malayalees reaching and settling in these cities continues to grow.

Networks and the Question of Identity of Malayalees

Migrants who arrive in new places are aliens with no dependable support to fall back. Such helplessness will be more serious in the case of pioneering migrants. The conditions of late entrants may not be so helpless apparently because the beachheads established by the earlier migrants, serve as anchors to hold on. Furthermore, earlier migrants would have created associations or unions in the new place. Such associations, termed as networks serve a very useful purpose in facilitating further migration. As Portes puts it, "once established such networks allow the migration to become self-sustaining and impervious to short term change in economic incentives".[16] With the help of such organisations, a three way interactional relationship between the host, the migrant group and the sending society may also evolve. In this triarchical relationship the sending society may also be in a position to influence the receiving society.[17]

The Malayalee migrants who moved to various parts of India created such networks in those places where they have set foot. Such organizations were started first in Madras, the earliest destination. One of the first organizations was the Madras Mahajana Sabha, started in 1884. It was an organization not only of the Malayalees, but also of other linguistic groups established for the purpose of securing more political privileges to the Indians. The earlier Malayalee organizations were those of the upper class people. The Malayalee Club organized in 1897 was the first of such organizations. The members were Pattar

Brahmins, and high caste Nairs who were holding lucrative and prestigious occupations. Another organization, the Kerala Club was started in 1912 mainly by Thiyyas. An important organization with larger representation of the middle and lower class people was the Kerala Samajam started in 1939. By 1940 the membership of the Samajam went up to 4,000. The Kerala Workers' Federation started in 1951 was another organization.[18] Since then, there was a mushroom growth of organizations and associations in all parts of Tamil Nadu.

Similar organizations of Malayalees were started in all the important cities where Malayalees had settled down. In Bombay the first of such organizations was the Nair Samajam started in 1921. The Kerala Samajam was started in Dadar in 1930.[19] The Kerala Club started in 1939 was the first organization of Delhi Malayalees. It was an organization of leading Malayalees of Delhi.[20] The Delhi Malayalee Association started in 1950 was an organization with wider representation. In Bangalore similar organizations were started from the forties. Similarly in all urban centres of India Malayalee/Kerala associations have come into existence. Of late confederations of such associations also have come into existence in various parts of India.

These organizations celebrate Onam and other festivals of Kerala. Various forms of cultural performances are also being staged on such occasions. They try to preserve the identity of Malayalees in those far away places and strive to render yeomen service to Malayalee settlers. Very often newcomers get solace and support in their trials and tribulations from such organistions..

Another important category of network is the sectarian organisation of different communities. Almost all the communities have established their separate associations in other parts of India. One of the earliest association of this category was the Malabar Muslim Association of Bangalore formed as far back as 1920.[21] Similarly, the Malabar Muslim Association was formed in Madras in 1940. The Catholics of Bombay, have organised Bombay Catholic Association in 1960.[22] In Bangalore, the Malayalee Catholics have formed their own organisation. Not to be left behind, the Hindus have formed Ayyappa Seva Sangham in Bangalore. Ayyappa Seva Sanghams have been opened up in almost all the important cities of India. These organizations render real yeomen service to the members belonging to their own communities. Mention may be made in this connection that the Malabar Muslim Association in Chennai renders help to the Hindus also by providing accommodation in the hostel under its ownership.

In addition to these sectarian associations separate places of worship are being opened up and maintained by different religious communities. The Marthomites were the first to open their own church in Bombay. The Jacobite Syrians followed suit by setting up their own place of worship in 1940.[23] Separate places of worship were established both by the Marthomites and Jacobites in Madras. In Delhi also these Christian sects have opened their own separate places of worship. The Syrian Catholics have not been far behind. They have set up their bishopric at Kalyan in Bombay. The St. Thomas parish in Bangalore is a major Syrian Catholic place of worship. All these Christian sects maintain their own separate churches and bishoprics in various other parts of India. The Hindus on their part have their own Ayyappa temples in different parts of India. Significantly, Lord Ayyappa is for practical purposes identified as a Malayalee daity. These sectarian religious institutions promote identity on religious basis. The secular networks like the Malayalee Associations are not so strong in comparison with the sectarian networks.

One of the avowed objectives of the innumerable Malayalee Associations is to preserve the identity of Malayalees in other parts of India. However, the endeavours to preserve the identity are being frustrated by various factors. No doubt, the nativist movement and the educational policies designed to satisfy the nativist demands are detrimental to the cause of the settlers. Nevertheless, they can serve as rallying points to maintain the identity of the settlers. However, they seem to be hesitant to come together in preserving their identity. Apparently, the reasons have to be sought in other factors including those connected with the settlement process. As a matter of fact, settlement is a social process leading to changes in the attitude and behavioural pattern of the migrants themselves. In so doing, they may shed some of their cultural heritage. At the same time, the second generation of the migrants comprises, for practical purposes, non migrants born and brought up in other parts of India. The peer group in the midst of which they grow consists mostly of non-Malayalees. The influence of the peer group in shaping the behavioural pattern and attitude of the adolescents is a well known fact. Needless to say, the peer group may imbibe the customs and mode of living of non-Keralites in the minds of the youngsters. As already mentioned, many among the second generation do not know how to read and write Malayalam, though they may be able to talk Malayalam. However, many of them seem to be disinclined to use Malayalam in their day to day communications. One needs not be surprised, if they sever their connections with Kerala in course of time and abandon Malayalam altogether. Endeavours to preserve the identity thus get frustrated.

Instead, there seems to be an inclination on the part of many Malayalees to assimilate at a quicker pace with the native population. This is in sharp contrast to what the ethnic communities like the Konkanis or Pattar Brahmins or even the tiny Gujarati community display in Kerala. The Konkani Brahmins who migrated to Kerala during the 16th century, scrupulously retain their language and customs though their habitat here is located at a distance of more than 1000 kms from Konkan region, their ancestral homeland. The Tamil Brahmins and Gujaratis also retain their identity. Why do Malayalees, who are familiar with this steadfast adherence to identity, are indifferent to it in their own case is a serious question.

Those ethnic groups who belonged to some compact communities clustered around certain particular localities only in the past. On the other hand, Malayalees are a heterogenous group divided into different castes and communities. Furthermore, their settlements in most parts of India are scattered in the midst of other linguistic communities. However, members of the ethnic communities like Konkanis now reside in the midst of other communities in Kerala. Even then they maintain their linguistic cum ethnic identity in tact. Apparently, there should be other reasons for the lukewarm attitude of Malayalees in this matter. It may perhaps be related to the cultural heritage of Malayalees. As a matter of fact, propensity to accept congeries of another culture is in a way related to the assimilation also. Certain communities accept cultural congeries and traits of other cultures diffused from outside at a quicker pace. The heritage of Keralites has been to adopt cultural congeries from outside without much hesitation. To cite an example, some of the items of food like *dosa and iddly* and types of dresses like sari and blouse are not of Kerala origin. They were introduced here only towards the closing decades of 19th century and Keralites adopted them as part of their culture at a quicker pace. This willingness to accept congeries from outside seems to have been the legacy of Kerala where a plural society, maintaining harmonious co-existence of different communities has been in existence for centuries. The inclination for assimilating in the new environment discernible among the Malayalees seems to be a continuation of such a cultural heritage. Perhaps the success of Malayalees to get on well with other linguistic groups not only in other parts of India, but also in other parts of the world stems from this heritage of theirs.

Notwithstanding the inclination for assimilation, the growth of the media can serve as a countervailing force at least for preserving the rudiments of Malayalee indentity. The leading Malayalam dailies publish their editions from some of the metropolitan cities of India. Similarly, the TV channels regularly relay Malayalam programmes even to foreign lands. How far, do the Malayalee settlers make use of these facilities is the question to be explored in this connection. Time alone can say whether the media can stem the tide and retrieve the lost ground.

Conclusion

In sum, most of the migrants from Kerala end up as settlers in other parts of India. The process of settlement which started in trickles gained momentum in course of time. Some of the settlers could occupy very high position at different periods of time. They include statesmen, politicians, administrators, professionals, academicians, artists, religious people and so on. Starting with Sir C. Sankaran Nair, who became the Member of the Viceroy's Executive Council and also the President of Indian National Congress, the galaxy of eminent Malayalees of foregone days include statesmen like V.K. Krishna Menon, who became a Defence Minister of India, administrators like Dr. John Mathai, who served as the Finance Minister of free India, scholar-cum-administrators like Sardar K.M. Panicker, artists like C. Sankara Pillai, freedom fighters like Barrister George Joseph, film star turned politicians like M.G. Ramachandran, diplomats like K.P.S. Menon and so on, to name only a few. Interestingly, Sir C. Sankaran Nair is reported to have told one Viceroy that the members of his family occupy the highest and the lowest office in India.[24] The highest office was in respect of his own position as the member of the Executive Council of the Viceroy and the lowest office was in respect of that of the village officer traditionally held by the members of his family. He himself and many others like him could occupy high positions, apparently because of their migration from the village moorings in Kerala.

The number of contemporary Malayalee settlers of high profile runs into hundreds of thousands of men and women. Some of the leading lights among them include the late K.R. Narayanan, Ex-President of India, P.C. Alexander, former Governor of Maharashtra, late J.N. Dixit, the diplomat, Ms. Jaya Jaitly, the Chairperson of Samata Party, Arundati Roy, the novelist, T.N. Seshan, the former Chief Election Commissioner, Dr. M.S. Swaminathan, the scientist, Dr. Madhava Menon, the legal luminary, Prakash Karat, the General Secretary of CPI (M) and so on. The ranks of Malayalee settlers also include hundreds of ordinary clerical staff working in various offices, nurses serving in the hospitals all over India, teachers working in different educational institutions, technicians of different trades, nuns in the convents, hotel workers, street-side vendors and hawkers and mere coolie workers besides the hundreds of thousands of defence personnel who guard the borders of India and valiantly face the insurgents in Kashmir and North East. They render exemplary service to the nation in their own humble capacity in every nook and cranny of India and many among them are able to win the goodwill of the people around them. Their position is somewhat similar to that of the unknown soldier whose role is as much important as that of the commander in winning the battle. They also enrich the state by sending remittances, though the amount is not as big as the remittances from the Gulf countries.

Notes and References

1. Piore, Michael J.: *Birds of Passage: Migrant Labour and Industrial Societies* (Cambridge University Press, 1979), p. 55.
2. Piore, Michael J.: *op.cit.* p. 52.
3. Piore, Michael J.: *op.cit.* p. 62.
4. Piore, Michael J.: *op.cit.* p. 60.
5. *Census of India 1991: Language Table.*
6. There were as many as 64622 Malayalam speaking people in Nilgiri district and 125601 in Kanyakumari district respectively in 1961. (See *Census of India 1961: Census Handbooks of Nilgiri and Kanyakumari districts*)
7. *Census of India 1991: Census Handbook of Greater Bombay.*
8. Myron, Weiner: *Sons of the Soil: Migration and Ethnic Conflict in India* (New Jersey, Princeton University Press, 1978), pp. 357-58.
9. Myron, Weiner: *op.cit.*, p. 42.
10. M.S. Gore: *Inmigrants and Neighbourhood* (Bombay, Tata Institute of Social sciences, 1970), p. 6.
11. Patel, G. Haribhai: "Keralite Migrant Female Labour in Fishing Units of Veravel City in Western India" in Vidyut Joshi (ed.) *Migrant Labour and Related Issues* (New Delhi, Oxford and I.B.H. 1987), pp. 180-81.
12. Piore, Michael J.: *op.cit.*, pp. 54-55.
13. Susan Lewandowski: *Migration and Ethnicity in Rural India: Kerala Migrants in the city of Madras 1870-1970* (Delhi, Manohar Publications, 1980), pp. 196-97.
14. Myron, Weiner: *op.cit.* pp. 266-67.
15. Myron Weiner: *op.cit.* p. 294.
16. Portes, Alejandro: "Economic Sociology and Sociology of Immigration: A Conceptual Overview" in Portes Alejandro (ed.) *The Economic Sociology of Immigration* (New York, Russell Sage Publications, 1995) p. 22.
17. Arthur, W. Helweg: "Indians in England" in M.S.A.Rao (ed.) *Studies in Migration* (Delhi, Manohar 1986), p. 365.

18. Susan Lewandowski: *op.cit.* pp. 148-159.
19. Susan Lewandowski: *op.cit.* pp. 192-93.
20. *Annual Report of Kerala Club, New Delhi, 1983.*
21. Thonippara, Francis: "Bangalore City and Malayalee Migration" in K.S. Mathew(ed); *Migration in South India* (Delhi, Sipra Publications, 2005) p. 62.
22. Susan Lewandowski, *op.cit.* p. 193.
23. Susan Lewandowski, *op.cit.* p. 192
24. K.P.S. Menon: *Sir C.Sankaran Nair* (Malayalam), (New Delhi, Government of India, Publication Division 1971), p. 6.

Chapter 7

Conclusions

Studies on migration from a historical angle are scanty, even though some of the migratory movements are events of historical importance. By themselves patterns of migration are capable of influencing and even reshaping further course of development. At the same time, as stated earlier, migration rarely occurs in pure form in nature but always in connection with other social processes. Studies on migration especially from a historical perspective have therefore to be within a broader framework of socio-economic and political development.

The present study was undertaken to uncover the migratory movements of Malayalees during the 20th century from a historical angle. Such a study was undertaken because no study on the migration of Keralites (Malayalees) from a historical angle appears to have been made, eventhough Malayalees are found in all parts of the world. In so far as migration from Kerala is concerned, it is for all practical purposes a twentieth century phenomenon. During the first half of the century, it was a development with a colonial legacy. With the attainment of independence of the colonies during the middle of 20th century migratory movements of the colonial period came to an end. Newer patterns emerged since then. Thus the study deals with the migratory movement from Kerala covering two phases: the colonial and post-colonial periods. A study on migration from Kerala cannot be made in isolation without examining the migratory movement in the country as a whole. Naturally, the present study covers the migration from Kerala within the context of the migratory movement in India.

After thus introducing the theme of the study, two main questions were posed in the next chapter on the beginning of the process of migration from Kerala. They are: (i) Why has there been no migratory movement from Kerala during nineteenth century, though millions of people had moved out of India to different parts of the world? (ii) How could migration originate form Kerala during the early decades of twentieth century? To start with, any pattern of migration is feasible under certain favourable conditions. The great transatlantic migration from Europe, for example could take place only after far reaching changes had taken place in the organisation of agriculture and industry. In India, where wantlessness in combination with occupational division of labour based on caste, prevailed for centuries as the core of the socio-economic fabric, no migration whatsoever was possible. Nevertheless, migration of millions of people took place under indenture system from different parts of India during the nineteenth century. Such a pattern of migration was rendered possible because, the Sirkar came forward and promoted it. Since the constraints in Kerala were still more stiff, practically nobody moved out of Kerala during nineteenth century.

Nevertheless, socio-economic transformation at a faster pace ensued in Kerala towards the closing decades of nineteenth century. Education which serves as a catalyzing agent in such changes had an earlier start in Kerala. Under the influence of modern ideas infused through education, the subsistence mindedness gave way to a development consciousness. With such a change in the attitude, an era of development ushered in Kerala during the early decades of twentieth century. Migratory movement also set in as a concomitant to the process of development.

Migration to foreign lands forms the theme of the Third Chapter. The important destinations of the millions of people who moved from India were Mauritius, Caribbean Islands, Guiana, South Africa, East Africa, Sri Lanka, Malaya, and Fiji. Myanmar, which was administered as part of India till 1935 was also an important destination. Emigrants from Kerala moved on a limited scale to Malaya, Burma (Myanmar) and Ceylon (Sri Lanka) only.

The country which attracted the largest number of migrants from India during the pre-independence period was Burma. The main reasons for it were the prospects for furthering ones economic prospects and the inclusion of Burma as part of India. However, anti-Indian sentiment began to surface in Burma from the early decades of the twentieth century. Most of the emigrants from India returned to India with great difficulty during the Japanese occupation. Those who returned to Burma after the War or those who remained in Burma were singled out and ill-treated by the Burmese authorities and as a consequence most of them opted to come back to India.

Migration from Kerala became brisk only when anti-Indian feeling was at its peak in Burma. Naturally, Malayalees could not become a numerically dominant group in Burma. Though migration from Kerala reached its peak level by 1931, the size of Malayalee population formed only 1.2 per cent of the Indian population in Burma. Most of the Keralites returned to India either during the Japanese occupation, or soon after the

independence of Burma. The majority of the Keralites in Burma were from Malabar region and most of them engaged in pretty trade.

Malaysia is perhaps the only country where the number of immigrants from India did not fall even after the withdrawal of British colonialism. Migration to Malayan peninsula started after the conquest of Penang in 1786. Traders, policemen and administrators were the early immigrants from India. Large scale migration took place after the opening of coffee, tea, rubber and oil palm plantations one after another in succession. Indian migrant workers were drawn mainly from Tamil and Telugu districts of the erstwhile Madras presidency. Keralites also started to move in fairly large numbers since the turn of the twentieth century. There was a slight fall in the size of Malayalee population since Malaya became independent in 1957. Though the overwhelming majority of the Indian population was engaged as coolie labourers, most of those from Kerala were employed in various categories of clerical, junior administrative, supervisory and technical posts. Nevertheless, there were a good number of coolie workers and petty hawkers from Kerala.

Ceylon is another country which attracted migrants from India right from the early decades of nineteenth century. Emigration from India was essentially a Tamil phenomenon. However, most of them were repatriated after the independence of Ceylon. Keralites were not many in Ceylon. Most of them were from Cochin and Malabar regions.

The Persian Gulf region became the promised land for a large number of emigrants from India during the second half of 20th century. Though on a limited scale, migration to the Gulf region started from the thirties, when a few oil companies were opened in the region. It became an exodus after the oil boom of 1970s. As seen earlier, nearly 2.8 million Indian workers were stated to be working in the beginning of 1990s in the Gulf countries like Saudi Arabia, United Arab Emirates, Bahrain, Kuwait, Oman and Qatar. Nearly half of them are stated to be from Kerala. The large scale migration from Kerala could be attributed to the widespread unemployment in combination with the age old trade-cum-ethnic connections of Kerala with the Gulf region. Immigrants to the Gulf countries are mostly unskilled and skilled workers drawn for a few years of service. Naturally, most of them proceed to the Gulf countries after leaving their families at home in Kerala. As a result, they remit a portion of their earnings to India. The remittances thus sent to Kerala constitute nearly 25 per cent of the state domestic product according to some estimates. The income thus accruing in Kerala through the inward remittances has become the main source for sustaining the conspicuous consumption which has emerged as part and parcel of the life style of the people of Kerala during recent years.

Though beginnings of migratory movements to many other parts of the world were made during the early decades of twentieth century, they did not gain momentum till the attainment of independence. The U.S.A. is one of the countries in which fairly large number of Keralites have migrated during recent years. Keralites form roughly 10 per cent of the ethnic Indian population in the U.S.A. Most of the migrants to the U.S.A. are well-educated persons. The list of other countries where fairly large number of Keralites have congregated includes Canada, Great Britain, West Germany, Australia and so on.

Internal migration to other parts of India was another pattern which gained momentum during the early decades of twentieth century. However, the process received a setback with the worldwide depression of the thirties. Though there was increase in the number of inmigrants, the percentage of the same as a ratio to the total population revolved around 2.5 till the outbreak of the Second World War. At the same time, opportunities for employment did not grow in sufficient numbers in any part of the country. Further, the linguistic and cultural barriers retarding migratory movements continued to remain strong in the country. Nevertheless, certain regions like Bihar, Uttar Pradesh, Rajasthan, Madras and Punjab emerged as areas with high intensity of migration. The regions which attracted inmigrants from other parts of India were Bengal, Assam, Bombay, Madhya Pradesh and Mysore.

However, during this period, migration from Kerala began to take an upward trend. Nevertheless, Kerala continued to remain as a net inmigrating region accommodating more inmigrants than sending outmigrants to other parts of India. A turning point came with the outbreak of the Second World War. With the outbreak of hostilities, demand for different categories of personnel for the army and other defence services went up very high in the country. Large number of young men from different parts of the country came forward and enrolled in the army. Migratory movement acquired a new dimension with the recruitment drive in the army. In the wake of these developments, Kerala became an outmigrating region. Youngmen from different parts of Kerala enrolled themselves in the army and moved to various parts of India. Comprehensive data relating to the migration from the three regions of Kerala are not available. Data relating to the Malayalee population living outside the present Kerala therefore become the only dependable source. The Malayalee population living outside Kerala region recorded an increase of more than ten times between 1901 and 1951, apparently because of the spurt in the migratory movement.

Various developmental programmes launched in independent India paved the way for the continued increase in the volume of internal migration. The percentage of inter-state migrants to the total population went upto 3.33 in 1961. The upward trend continued during the sixties and seventies. However, the census data of 1991 point to a declining trend in the tempo of migratory movement. Shrinking employment opportunities in combination with the emergence of nativist sentiment in states like Tamil Nadu, Maharashtra, Assam, Karnataka seems to have put a check to the rising tempo of internal migration.

The upward trend in the migratory movement from Kerala continued during fifties and sixties. However, intensity of outmigration seemed to have reached the peak level by 1971. Since then, the trend in the flow of outmigration seems to be on the decline. However, the declining trend has been counterbalanced by an increase in the flow of external migration. By 1980, the number of external migrants has surpassed the number of internal migrants apparently because of the opening to the Gulf region.

The profiles of the migrants from Kerala have been superior to those of the other ethnic groups from the very beginning. Majority of the migrants from Kerala were in the age group 15-34 both in the case of males and females. The proportion of the young children and old people among the migrants was much lower than that of the population of the country as a whole.

Since migrants from Kerala move to the regions where languages other than their mother tongue are spoken they have to be proficient in more than one language. The proportion of the migrants speaking other languages as a subsidiary language was well over 60 per cent. English is used as a subsidiary language by the migrants in all parts of India. However, the proportion of the people speaking Tamil as a subsidiary language was the highest apparently because migrants in Tamil Nadu and Karnataka, the two leading inmigrating states of Keralites, use Tamil instead of English. Marathi, the regional language of Bombay was spoken as a subsidiary language by an insignificant percentage of the migrants. Similarly, Kannada, the regional language of Karnataka did not figure as the single largest subsidiary language with the migrants from Kerala in Karnataka. The percentage of people using Hindi as a subsidiary language was fairly high in cities like Bombay and Delhi.

Throughout history, male migrants outnumbered females. Ratio of the male migrants from Kerala was the highest among the states in India. The latest trend is for a fall in the male ratio as more females, also opt to migrate. Similarly, majority of the migrants have moved to the urban areas. Percentage of migrants from Kerala to the urban areas was the highest among the migrants in India.

What happened to the migrants forms the theme of Chapter Six. Most of them who were mere sojourners in the beginning eventually settled down in various parts of India. The process of settlement involves changes in the original plans as well as behavioural pattern of the migrants. Though migrants have settled down in almost all parts of India, the overwhelming majority are in Karnataka, Tamil Nadu and Maharashtra. By and large, migration is an urbanward movement in all parts of the world. In sharp contrast to this pattern, a good proportion of the migrants from Kerala have moved and settled down in the rural areas of Tamil Nadu and Karnataka. It was mainly the peasant farmers and agricultural labourers from Kerala who settled down in the rural tracts of Dakshina Kannada and Kodagu districts of Karnataka state and Kanyakumari and Nilgiri districts of Tamil Nadu.

The migrant settlers to the urban areas who moved mainly for the purpose of employment took up various kinds of occupations in other parts of India. Most of them have been employed in various categories of service activities in which they could secure proportionately more number of jobs in comparison with other linguistic groups. Though female migration has been rising steadily, only a minority of them moved for the purpose of employment. In a sense, the migration of the females was by and large incidental to the process of settlement to which nearly half of the females seem to have opted by migrating for the purpose of marriage.

Most of the migrants in India take up occupations other than agriculture. By and large, the percentage of the migrants employed in other services was the highest followed by manufacturing activities. (However, trade and commerce formed the occupation with the largest percentage of migrants from Gujarat and Rajasthan. Fairly large percentage of Bengalis were employed as cultivators.) With the largest percentage of the migrant workers employed in other services, the all India pattern holds good in the case of migrants from Kerala. Significantly, the Malayaless, in "the other services" could make a name for themselves in various parts of India.

The Malayalee migrants who settled in other parts of India face a number of problems. Non-availability of Kerala type of food, inadequacy of housing facilities, difficulties for communication with the neighbourhood on account of language barriers are some of the problems to be encountered. Difficulty for educating the children in Malayalam and securing marriage partners of Malayalee origin are some other problems.

Added to these problems of adjustments, they have to put up with the unfriendly attitude of the host society in various parts of India. Nativist movement which gained importance in some parts of India became suspicious and even hostile towards the migrant settlers from other parts of India. Some of the nativist organisations like the Shiv Sena took a path of violent agitation against the Malayalees a few years back. Though the open hostility has subsided it may flair up at any time. Some of the measures adopted by the state governments designed to placate the demands of the nativists are detrimental to the interests of the Malayalee settlers. Nevertheless, there is not much fall in the magnitude of migration or settlement of the migrants.

The Keralites who migrated to various parts of India have opened their own clubs, associations and schools. Some of the associations are very old. The Malayalee Association in Madras is more than 100 years old. The Delhi Malayalee Association was formed in 1939. They celebrate *Onam* and various cultural activities dear to Malayalees. Not only organisations and cultural activities but also places of worship of their own have been established by them. The Orthodox Syrian Christians and Marthoma Syrian Christians were the first to open such exclusive places of worship of their own. In Delhi, Bombay and other metropolitan cities both the sects have their own bishoprics and parishes. The Syrian Catholics also followed the example of the other two sects and opened their own bishoprics and exclusive places of worship of their own in Bombay and other places. The Hindus on their own part have opened Ayyappa Samajams and Ayyappa Temples. The Muslims are the only group who do not have their own exclusive places of worship, though they have opened Kerala Muslism Associations in various places outside Kerala. These institutions and organisations have been operating as networks providing yeomen service to the inmigrants. While promoting the welfare of the inmigrants in those places where the organisations were working, they were striving to retain the cultural and ethnic identities of Malayalees in different parts of India.

However, the endeavours at preserving the identity are being frustrated for various reasons. The second generation of the settlers appears to be lukewarm to preserve their Malayalee identity. At the same time, assimilation with the host society at a faster rate seems to be the trend among most of the Malayalee settlers. The developments of the media like newspaper and television may perhaps retrieve the ground at least in preserving the rudiments of identity.

In retrospect, nearly one hundred years have elapsed since migratory movements of the Keralites became fairly widespread. Migration to foreign lands and to the other parts of India could serve as a safety valve to the growing number of unemployed youths of Kerala. The remittances which the migrants sent have been instrumental in supporting many families and in improving the standard of living of the people at large. Remittances are not merely from the Gulf countries but also from other parts of India. According to the Rural Debt and Investment Survey of 1961-62, 16 per cent of the households in Kerala were getting on an average Rs.390 per year by way of remittances from their members working in other parts of India.[1] Interestingly, even during the thirties of 20th century, remittances were flowing, though on a moderate scale into some villages in Cochin from where emigration had taken place to other countries.[2] The life style in Kerala has been transformed far beyond recognition by all standards. It is the remittances which provide the much needed material resources for such a transformation.

A far more important issue is the future of the migrants from Kerala in far off places and the future of migration per se. The emerging scenario in the country forbodes of an unhealthy future in so far as the future of the migrants are concerned. The nativist movement which gained prominence in some parts of India stands for narrow regional interests, very often at the cost of national interests. Some of the state governments in turn have taken various steps designed to satisfy the nativists. Some of them are not only harmful to the interests of the inmigrants but also capable of undermining the constitutional safeguards extended to the minorities including inmigrants. Those steps in conformity to the political demands of the nativists are, in the words of Myron Weiner, "directed less at facilitating linguistic assimilation than at discouraging migration".[3] Not surprisingly, a declining trend has set in, in the whole process of inter-state migration. However, the fall in numbers in internal migration is being compensated by the spurt in the number of Malayalees opting to move to pastures new like the Gulf countries and the U.S.

Nevertheless, the pace of permanent settlement in the foreign lands is rather slow apparently as the Gulf countries where more than 80 per cent of the Malayalee migrants work, do not allow foreigners to become permanent settlers. Among the foreign countries, which allow migrants to become permanent settlers, the US stands first, where a fairly large number of Malayalee migrants have settled. Canada, Australia and some west European countries have also become the haven of a few thousand Malayalees. The pioneering attempts at migration of Nayarsan (A.M. Nair) in Japan or Malabari Muslims in Indonesia have not been successful in attracting Malayalees mainly on account of the anti-immigration policies of those countries. In sum, it is the absence of positive conditions which stand in the way of Malayalees from migrating and settling down in large numbers in other parts of the world.

Notes and References

1. "All India Rural Debt and Investment Survey 1961-62 – Current Resources of Rural Households", See *Reserve Bank of India Bulletin*, December 1965.
2. T.K. Sankara Menon: *Report of the Economic Survey in Various Villages of Cochin State* (Ernakulam, Government Press, 1935).
3. Myron Weiner: *Sons of the Soil: Migration and Ethnic Conflict in India* (New Jersey, Princeton University Press, 1978), p. 335.

Bibliography

Aiya, Nagam V., *Travancore State Manual, Vol.III* (Trivandrum, Government Press, 1905).

Andrews, K.P. (ed.), *Keralites in America* (New York, Glen Oaks, Literary, Market Review, 1983).

Anstey, Vera, *The Economic Development of India* (London, Longman Green & Co.,1936).

Arasarathnam, Sinnappa, *Indians in Malaysia and Singapore* (London, Institute of Race Relations, 1970).

Birks, J.S. and Sinclair, C.A., *Arab Manpower: The Crisis of Development* (New York, St.Martins Press, 1980).

Berliner, Joseph, S., "Internal Migration: A Comparative Disciplinary View" in Brown Allen (ed.) *Internal Migration: A Comparative Perspective* (New York, Academic Press, 1977).

Chandan Amarjit, *Indians in Britain* (New Delhi, Sterling Publishing Co. 1986).

Chakravarti, N.R., *Indian Minority in Burma* (Oxford University Press, 1971).

Daniels, Roger, "The Indian Diaspora in the United States" in Judith Brown (ed.), *Migration: The Asian Experience* (Oxford, St Martin's Press, 1994).

Davis, Kingsley, *Population of India and Pakistan* (New Jersey, Princeton University Press, 1951).

Delhi Directory of Kerala (New Delhi, Dravida Publications, 1996).

Fisher, Maxine P., *The Indians in New Yori City* (New delhi, Heritage Publishers, 1980).

Gangulee, N., *Indians in Empire Overseas: A Survey* (London, New India Publishing House, 1947).

Gillon K.S., *Fiji's Indian Migrants* (Melbourne, Oxford University Press, 1962).

Gopalan, A.K., *In the Cause of the People: Reminiscences* (Bombay Orient Longman, 1973).

Handlin, Oscar, *The Uprooted: The Epic Story of Great Migration that Made the American People* (New Delhi, Asian Book, 1973).

Hill, Poly, *Migrant Cocoa Farmer of Southern Ghana* (Cambridge University Press, 1976).

Innes, C.A., *Madras District Gazetteers: Malabar and Anjengo* (Madras, Superintendent, Government Press, 1908).

Jha, J.C., *Aspects of Indentured Inland Emigration in North East India 1889-1908* (New Delhi, Indus Publishing Company, 1996).

Jansen Clifford, J., *Readings in the Sociology of Migration* (London, Pergamon Press, 1970).

Jeffrey, Robin, *The Decline of Nayar Dominance* (New Delhi, Vikas Publishing House, 1976)

Jensen, Joan, *Passage from India: Asian Indian Immigrants in North America* (New Haven, Yale University Press, 1973).

Joseph, K.V., *Migration and Economic Development of Kerala* (Delhi, Mittal Publications, 1988).

—— *Culture and Industrial Development:The Indian Experience* (New Delhi,Anmol Publications, 2004)

Kannan K.P. and Hari K.S., "Kerala's Gulf Connection: Remittances and Macro-economic Impact" in K.C.Zachariah (ed.) *Kerala's Gulf Connection* (Trivandrum, Centre for Development Studies, 2002).

Karoor, Isaac, "History of Keralite Immigration in United States" in Andrews K.P., *op.cit.*

Kurien, Raju, *Patterns of Migration from Kerala* (Trivandrum, M.Phil Dissertation, Centre for Development Studies, 1976).

Kondapi, C., *Indians Overseas: 1838-1949* (Oxford University Press, 1951).

Lee, Everett, S., "A Theory of Migration" in *Demography* Vol.3, No.3, 1966.

Lewandowski, Susan, *Migration and Ethnicity in Urban India* (Delhi, Manohar, 1980).

Madhavan M.C., "Dimensions of Indian Emigration", *The Hindu*, Feb.1985.

Mathew, K.S., Singh, Mahavir and Varkey Joy (Ed.), *Migration in South India* (Delhi, Shipra Publications, 2005).

Mc Gee, T.G., "Rural Labour Mobility in South and South East Asia" in William H Mc Neill (ed.) *Human Migration Patterns and Policies* (Indiana University Press, 1978).

Michael, J. Piore, *Birds of Passage: Migrant Labour and Industrial Societies* (Cambridge University Press, 1979).

Mana Saud Al Otiba, *Petroleum and the Economy of the United Arab Emirates* (London, Croom Helm, 1977).

Moch, Leslie Page, "Moving Europeans: Historical Migration Practices in Western Europe" in Robin Cohen (ed.) *Cambridge Survey of World Migration* (Cambridge University Press, 1995).

Menon, Achutha, C., *Cochin State Manual* (Ernakulam, Cochin Sircar Press, 1911).

Menon, Kesava K.P., *Bilathi Vishesham* (Mal.) (Information on Europe, Kozhikode, Mathrubhoomi Printing and Publishing Works, 1983).

Menon, K.P.S., *C.Sankaran Nair* (Malayalam) (New Delhi, Govt. of India, Ministry of Information and Broadcasting, 1971).

Mayer, Adrian, C., *Land and Society in Malabar* (Bombay, Oxford University Press, 1952).

Mukerjee, Radha Kamal, *Foundations of Indian Economics* (London, Longman Green and Co., 1916).

Myrdal, Gunnar, *Asian Drama* (New York, Pantheon Press, 1968).

—— *Economic Theory of Underdevelopment* (London, Gerald Duckworth & Co. Ltd., 1957).

Nair, A.M., *Jappanil Anpathi Anchu Varsham* (Malayalam, Autobiography of A.M.Nair, Kottayam, D.C.Books, 1982).

Nair, Gopinathan P.R., *Asian Emigration to the Middle East: Emigration from India* (Trivandrum, Unpublished Working Paper, Centre for Development Studies, 1983).

Narayana, M.R., "Patterns of Regional Migration in India 1961-1981" in *Journal of Indian School of Political Economy*, Vol.V, No.4.

Nayyar, Deepak, "International Labour Migration from India: A Macro-Economic Analysis" in Rashed Amjad, *To the Gulf and Back* (New Delhi, I.L.O. Asian Employment Programme, 1989).

Panchanan, Saha, *Repatriation of Indian Labour 1834-1900* (New Delhi, People's Publishing House, 1970).

Paul, P. Louis, "Early Immigrants" in K.P.Andrews (ed.) *op.cit.*

Pazheparambil, Thomas: *Swapnabhoomiyil* (Mal: In Dreamland) (Muvattupuzha Mar Mathews Press, 1978).

Portes Alejandro Deo, "Economic Sociology and Sociology of Immigration" in Portes Alejandro (ed.) *The Economic Sociology of Immigration* (New York, The Sage Foundation 1995).

Piplai, Tapan; Majumdar Niloy, "Internal Migration in India: Some Scoio-economic Implications" in *Samkhya*, Series B, Vol.31, 1969.

Ravenstein, E.G., "Laws of Migration" in *Journal of Royal Statistical Society*, 1885.

Pramati, Datta, "Inter-state Migration in India", *Margin*, 18.

Rajoo, R., "Indians in Peninsular Malaya" in I.J. Bahadur Singh (ed.) *Indians in South East Asia* (New Delhi, Sterling Publishers, 1982).

Redford, Arthur, *Labour Migration in England 1800-1850* (Manchestor, Manchestor University Press, 1926).

Rao, M.S.A., *Studies in Migration* (Delhi, Manohar, 1986).

Singh, Shubha, *Overseas Indians - The Global Family* (Delhi, Shipra Publications, 2005)

Sjastad, Larry, S., "The Cost of Returns of Human Migration" in *Journal of Political Economy*, Oct. 1962, Part II.

Skeldon, R., "On Migration Patterns in India during 1970s" in *Population and Development Review*, Vol.12.

Sandhu, Kernial Singh, *Indians in Malaya* (Cambridge at the Cambridge University Press, 1969).

Shea, Thomas W., "Barriers to Economic Development in Traditional Societies Malabar: A Case Study" in *Journal of Economic History*, Vol.19, 1959.

Prejor, Robin J., Integrating International and Internal Migration Theories in Mery M.Krutz (ed.) *Global Trends in Migration: Theory and Research.* (New York Centre for Migration Studies, 1986).

Shirras, Findlay, "Indian Migration", Walter Willcox (ed.) *International Migration*, Vol.II, *Interpretations* (New York, Golden Reach Publishers, 1969).

Singh, Surjit, "Indian Immigrants to Canada" in *The Indian Journal of Labour Economics,* Vol.41, No.4, 1998.

Timberg, Thomas A., *The Marwaris from Traders to Industrialists* (New Delhi, Vikas Publishing House, 1978).

Tinker, Hugh, *The Baniyan Tree: Overseas Emmigrants from India, Pakistan and Bangladesh* (London, Oxford University Press, 1977).

Todaro, M.P., "A Model of Labour Migration and Urban Unemployment in Less Developed Countries" in *American Economic Review*, March 1969.

Thomas, Brinley, *International Migration and Economic Development: A Trend Report and Bibliography* (Paris, Unesco, 1961).

Thundy, P.Zacharias, "Keralites in America: Search for a New Identity", K.P. Andrew, *op.cit.*

Valavanthara, Antony, *India in 1500 AD: Translation of the Narratives of Joseph, the Indian* (Mannanam, Rishi Institute 1984), p.184.

Wikramasinghe, Nira, "Migration and Otherness in Sri Lanka" in Crispin, Bates (ed.), *Community, Empire and Migration:South Asians in Diaspora* (New York, Palmgrave 2001).

Ward and Conner, *Geographical and Statistical Memoirs of the Survey of Travancore and Cochin States* (Trivandrum, Government Press, 1863).

Weiner, Myron, "International Migration and Development: Indians in the Persian Gulf" in *Populaiton and Development Review*, Vol.5, No.1, March 1982.

Weiner, Myron, *Sons of the Soil: Migration and Ethnic Conflict in India* (New Jersey, Princeton University Press, 1978).

Wood, Charles, H., "Equilibrium and Historical Structural Perspective on Migration" in *International Migration Review* Vol.16, 1982.

Watts, Maurice Emigdius, "Travancore" in *Asiatic Review*, Vol.XXVI, 1930.

Zachariah, K.C., *A Historical Study of Internal Migration in the Indian Sub-Continent - 1901-1931* (Bombay, Asia Publishing House, 1964.

—— "Migration and Population Growth" in Kurup, R.S. and George K.A. (ed.) *Population Growth in Kerala* (Trivandrum, Demographic Research Centre, 1965).

—— *Migration in Greater Bombay* (Bombay, Asia Publishing House, 1968).

Zachariah, K.C., Mathew, E.T. and Irudaya Rajan, S.: *Impact of Migration on Kerala's Economy and Society* (Trivandrum, Centre for Development Studies, Working Paper No.297, 1999).

Zelinskey, Wilbur, "Hypothesis on Mobility Transition" in *Geographical Review* 61, 1971.

Iyer, Subramanian G., *Some Economic Aspects of British Rule in India* (Madras, Swadeshi Mitram Press, 1903).

Brown Judith (ed), *Migration; The Asian Experience.* (Oxford, St. Marin's Pres,1994).

B. Government Publications

Government of the Princely State of Cochin (G.O.C.): *Census Reports for the years 1891, 1901, 1911, 1921, 1931 and 1941* (Ernakulam, Superintendent Census Operations, Cochin State).

—— *Notes in the Economic Survey of Cochin State* (Ernakulam, Superintendent, Census Operations, Cochin State).

—— *Report of the Economic Survey of Nayarambalam Village, Anthikad Village, Chundal Village, Vallivattam Village, Vadama Village etc.* (Ernakulam, T.K. Sankara Menon, Superintendent, Economic Survey, Cochin State, 1935).

Government of India (G.O.I), *Census of India 1901*, Vol.XII, *A Burma Part II, Imperial Tables.*

—— *Census of India 1901, Vol.XI, Bombay Town and Island Part VI.* Tables - Table X, Languages.

—— *Report of the Committee of Emigrants from India to the Crown Colonies and Protectorates* (London, Sanuderson Committee, 1911).

—— *Report of the Census of India 1921, Imperial Tables* (New Delhi, Registrar General and Census Commissioner).

—— *Census of India 1921, Vol.X, Burma, Part I Report, Subsidiary Tables.*

—— *Census of India 1931, Vol.II, Imperial Tables.*

—— *Review of Trade of India* (Calcutta, Government Press, 1932).

—— *Report of the Census of India 1951, Paper I, Languages* (New Delhi, Registrar General and Census Commissioner of India, 1959).

—— *Census of India 1951 Working Population of Calcutta Industrial Region by Industry Place of Birth and Educational Attainment.*

—— *Census of India 1961, Part II C, Cultural Tables.*

—— *Census of India 1961, Part II C (IV) Migration Tables.*

—— *Census of India 1971, Part II (C) Social and Cultural Tables.*

—— *Census of India 1971, Part II (D) Migration Tables.*

—— *Census of India 1971, Part II* D.3, *Migration to Urban Centres* having 100,000 and above population.

—— *Census of India 1981, Series I India, Part V A&B VIII Migration Tables.*

—— *Geographic Distribution of Internal Migration 1971-1981* (New Delhi, 1989).

—— *Census of India 1991, Part V D, Series D.3, Migration Tables.*

Government of Kerala (G.O.K.): *Report of Housing and Employment Survey 1980* (Trivandrum, Directorate of Economics and Statistics).

—— *Census of 1961, Kerala, Economic Tables.*

Govt. of India (G.O.I.) *Census of India 1961, Vol.XIX, Delhi, Part II C, Cultural and Migration Tables.*

Govt. of Maharashtra, *Census of India 1961, Vol.X, Maharashtra Part X (1-C), Greater Bombay: Special Migration Tables.*

Govt. of Madras Presidency, *Census Reports for the years 1871, 1881, 1891, 1901, 1911, 1921, 1931 and 1941.*

—— *Report of the South India Planters' Enquiry Committee 1896* (Madras, Superintendent, Govt. Press).

—— *Report of Indian Emigrants to Ceylon and Malaya, 1917* (Madras, Superintendent, Govt. Press).

Govt. of Madras State, *Census of India 1961, Vol.IX, Madras, Part V(ii), Special Migration Tables.*

Govt. of Madras Presidency, *Report of the Malabar Tenancy Committee 1940* (Madras, Superintendent, Government Press).

—— *Statistical Appendix to the District Gazetteer of South Canara District* (Madras, Superintendent, Govt. Press).

Govt. of Madras State, *Census of 1951* (a) *District Census Handbook of Malabar District* (b) *District Census Handbook of South Canara District.*

Govt. of the Princely State of Mysore: *Census of India 1921, Vol.XXIII, Mysore, Part I Report.*

—— *Census Report of 1931* (Mysore State, 1931).

—— *Census of India 1941, Part XXII,Mysore, paper I Report.*

Government of Mysore State: *Census of India 1951, Mysore State Part I, Report.*

Government of the Princely State of Travancore: *Census Reports of Travancore for the years 1875, 1881, 1891, 1901, 1911, 1921, 1931 and 1941.*

—— *Report of the Unemployment Committee 1928.*

Govt. of Travancore-Cochin State, *Report of the Census of 1951.*

Govt.of the Princely State of Travancore: *Report of the Administration of Travancore 1942-43* (Trivandrum, Government Press, 1943).

Reserve Bank of India, All India Rural Debt and Investment Survey 1961-62: Current Resources of Rural Households (See R.B.I. Bulletin, Dece. 1965.

C. Archives Materials

G.O. Nos. 547-48/Public dated 1.6.1901 of the Govt. of Madras.

G.O.No. 377/Public dated 17.5.1907 of the Government of Madras.

G.O.No. 406/Public dated 14.5.1908 of Government of Madras.

G.O.No. 966-67/Public dated 20.9.1901 of Government of Madras.

G.O.No. 870/Public dated 30.9.1903 of Government of Madras.

Notes connected with G.O.No. 635/Public dated 23.5.1913.

G.O.No. 655/Public dated 23.5.1913 of Government of Madras.

G.O.No. 803/Public dated 27.6.1913 of Government of Madras (All from Archives Madras).

Government of India Foreign and Political Department, Secret External Proceedings Nos. 46-54 dated March 1921 (Archives, New Delhi).

Simla Records, Government of India, Foreign Department, External A - Proceedings No.6-8 of September 1903 (Archives, New Delhi).

Proceedings No. 52 - Telegraph dated 11th (received 16th) 1919 from His Majestys' Secretary to State for India, London to His Excellency the Viceroy, Simla (Archives, New Delhi).

Index